WAKING WISDOM

WAKING WISDOM

What the Cat Saw

KIM PARKER

EUROPA

Europa Centre

Copyright © 2021 by Kim Parker
All rights reserved. No part of this book may be reproduced in any form by mechanical or electronic means, including information storage and retrieval systems, without permission in writing from the publisher, except by a reviewer or researcher who may quote brief passages in a review or scholarly publication with author credits. Every effort to comply with copyright requirements has been made by seeking permission and acknowledging owners of source material used in the text.

Disclaimer:
i) This book is a collection of memories.The personal stories and memories by individuals recorded here are their version of events and have been both provided and reproduced in good faith with no disrespect or defamation intended. Every effort has been made to ensure the researched information is correct. No liability for incorrect information or factual errors will be accepted by the author.
ii) The views and opinions expressed in this work are solely those of the author. Some names may have been changed to protect privacy; however, they reflect real people and events.

Publishing Details:

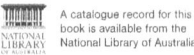

Publisher: Europa Centre
Editor: Eddie Albrecht, Pickawoowoo Publishing Group
Cover Artist: Laila Savolainen Pickawoowoo Publishing Group
Design/Formatting: Pickawoowoo Publishing Group / www.pickawoowoo.com
Printing and distribution: Lightning Source (USA, UK, AUS, EUR).

ISBN: 978-0-6451736-0-4 (paperback)
ISBN: 978-0-6451736-1-1 (ebook)

A catalogue record for this book is available from the National Library of Australia

Praise for Waking Wisdom Book 1

"The buzz word in paranormal research at present is consciousness. The author succinctly illustrates her own very interesting views on this matter, often through her own experiences. There is much food for thought within this book along with, I am pleased to say, humour."

Tricia Robertson, past President of the Scottish Society for Psychical Research, Lecturer, Researcher, Broadcaster and Author; Things You Can do When You're Dead. More Things You Can do When You're Dead. It's Life and Death, but Not as You Know It.

* * *

This very special memoir is a feast of short reminiscences about the various non-ordinary events – synchronicities, encounters with human and animal spirits, precognitive dreams, shamanic engagements – experienced by Kim in her life's journey. We read with a growing sense of wonder and thrill of recognition as we too begin to sense the possibilities of border-crossing between our embodied selves and infinite consciousness as it manifests in the everyday. The goal of this beautifully written book is to help us (after Silver

Birch) to widen our tiny, socially conditioned windows of perception to glimpse the vast vibrational universe of which we are a part. To learn to gain, as she has, "a vastly broadened appreciation of what it means to be loved beyond all measure, cherished, conscious and eternally connected to the web of being." Kim weaves together theories and cultural traditions drawn from a life lived as a shaman, medium, dream interpreter, and teacher. Her ontological relationship to these events is never at issue – Kim's is a truly authentic, heartful voice. This small miracle of a book models the translation of the everyday self into a fuller and higher version of being for readers at all stages of their spiritual journeys.

Tamar Gordon, Anthropologist - Rensselaer Polytechnic Institute

* * *

Kim Parker has a gift for story telling. Through this wonderful volume we catch a glimpse of the world of the shaman, the non-ordinary world where dreams convey messages, after-death contacts bring peace and reassurance and everyday contacts are full of meaningful synchronicities. Simply written, with engaging honesty and down to earth practical observations, the twenty four stories in this book will expand your sense of possibility. It is a wonderful book for anyone open to the realisation that behind the mundane of our everyday life, the world is more magical than we can possibly

imagine.
We love, love, love this book.

Victor and Wendy Zammit - Co-authors of The Friday Afterlife Report

Contents

Praise For Waking Wisdom Book 1 — v

Introduction — 2

1. What The Cat Saw — 5
2. Tea Drop Teachings — 9
3. The First Giggle — 14
4. Nagged From Beyond The Grave — 22
5. Dogs, Books and Mystical Moments — 28
6. Shamans, Dogs and The Afterlife — 34
7. Huntsman Spider Message — 44
8. Hearing Voices, Rasputin and Fish — 50

9	What's In A Name?	55
10	Feathers, Feathers Everywhere	58
11	There is a Snake in My Marriage Basket	65
12	My Cosmic Gift Of Ancient Wisdom Cards	70
13	It's a Giving World	76
14	The Heart Of Things	80
15	The Oddest Thing	83
16	Look Away	87
17	An Interesting Week	97
18	Oneness, Dreams and Waterlilies	104
19	A Confluence of Kindnesses	111
20	Charm	120
21	The Gate Keeper	123
22	The Universal Science Group	127

| 23 | The Quantum Altar of Availability | 131 |
| 24 | Dad, Books and Dreams | 134 |

About The Author 143

Wisdom, sapience, or sagacity, is the ability to think and act using knowledge, experience, understanding, common sense and insight. Wisdom is associated with attributes such as unbiased judgment, compassion, experiential self-knowledge, self-transcendence and non-attachment, and virtues such as ethics and benevolence. *(Source : Wikipedia)*

WAKING WISDOM

WARRANTS

WELLNESS

(warrants: as in protects, safeguards and guarantees)

Introduction

Sharing life experiences can create emotional cohesion, invite discussion and touch our hearts, minds and souls on multiple frontiers.

Story telling is one of the oldest arts. Oral traditions, pre-dating written language, kept a community or tribe's history alive, their values and their concepts of the sacred current. Tales that are told entertain and are an effective mechanism for knowledge transfer because they inform. They instruct us how to act wisely, to understand our place in the greater scheme of things and assist us to comprehend the perspectives of others.

People have been telling tales and listening to tales as far back as we know. In some cases stories were considered so valuable that they could be given to others as gifts or made as offerings.

When our brains hear a story that captures attention, the neurons fire in the same pattern as the speaker's brain, this is known as neural coupling. The brain can respond to captivating stories as if they were actually happening to the listener.

'Mirror neurons' create coherence between a speaker's brain and the brains of his/her audience members. (Why Storytelling Works: The Science, Ariel group.)

Emotionally touching stories can actually increase the production of oxytocin, which in turn increases our generosity and compassion. Therefore stories can affect our behaviour in addition to creating new perspectives of our experience of reality.

In a global technological storm of information, life experiences and their sharing, guide us to the heart of what is of great importance, what truly matters to us as individuals and as a species.

There is little difference really between a story and a tale, perhaps the big difference is that a story tends to have a definite path, a goal and a hero or heroine. Tales however, from my life experience of over sixty years of the non-ordinary are akin to being thrown to the four winds. Tales take us on wild rides into the very essence of the previously unknown or unacknowledged. The path is more a spiral than it is linear. Tales challenge our sense of what is real and laugh in the face of our mortal beliefs. They mock our narrow sense of what is possible. However, when you allow the imagination to wander through a tale as if it were your own it grants gifts that expand the conscious understanding of reality. A good tale can thrill you to the core as it unfurls before you the inherent possibilities hidden deep within your own consciousness.

There are many tales of my personal life experiences collected here. They are for perusal by those who refuse to be restricted to a life that is reduced to a reflection of the material world only. This book is for hearts that thirst for the miraculous, for a spiritual life that isn't just dogma, for a science of being that incorporates rather than scorns the extraordinary.

The very different types of experiences indicate that such happenings cannot always, or even often, be replicated in a science laboratory. They are frequently spontaneous and not orchestrated by the person who experiences them. Science does not have procedures and protocols to test for such events and hence they are pushed aside as being unable to be substantiated. The value of human testimony by reliable witnesses is ignored no matter the similarities, consistencies and durability of those testimonies over time and throughout vastly differing cultures.

My advice, if required, is to wander through these tiny tales as if you were living them. Question what would change in you if these things had truly been your experiences. What beliefs would be laid aside as uncomplimentary to you as a spiritual being of immortal consciousness? Watch the light of expanding perspectives shining around the harsh corners of societal conditioning. What self-limiting guilts and blames, shames and judgements would you throw into the abyss? Lay aside scorn and ridicule and let your mind fly free. Find and cherish the shiny nuggets of possibility nurtured in the realms of the non-ordinary human experience.

Most of all enjoy these gifts from my heart to yours.

Chapter 1

What The Cat Saw

This tiny tale tends to support the theory that energy itself has consciousness. It suggests that life is an agreement process in which energy creates forms at levels we have yet to even approach understanding. Additionally, the science behind such agreements and arrangements is not even close to being within our grasp.

Cats have been companions of mine since my earliest memories of dressing the long-suffering Mandy, a tortoiseshell cat, in dolls' clothes and pushing her around in the dolls' pram. Anyone who has led a life accompanied by cats will probably have experienced the behaviour I am about to describe. Very few I suspect have had the great good fortune to perceive the cause of that behaviour. I passed more than sixty years in the company of cats before one cat introduced me to ten seconds of another reality.

Every now and then a cat's pupils will become huge and dark as they appear to see something in the room that we can't see. They will twist their heads around following this invisible form, or even chase it around the house. What I have until recently called the cat crazies, often lead to mishaps such as broken things, curtain climbing and plain odd behaviour that the cats in question would not normally exhibit.

Like everyone else no doubt, I have always put such bizarre behaviour down to the inherent nature of cats. Sometimes we think of it as naughtiness or boredom or even curiosity. The latter was blamed for the demise of a large Chinese vase I kept by the front door. After years of not paying it any attention one of our cats decided to stand on his hind legs and pop his head in the vase and bring it toppling to its doom on the ceramic tiles in the entry foyer. However, my opinion of the cause of the cat crazies altered when I experienced something rather strange.

In the house where I live there are two terracotta elephants on low lying ledges either side of a very short passageway between the kitchen and the lounge room. The cats have never, ever climbed on them in the few years of our joint residence. They never paid these elephants any attention whatsoever. Until one day the cat in the lounge room with me got an apparent attack of the cat crazies. Her eyes went dark and she very obviously thought she could see something in the room.

Unfortunately, that something she thought she could see was hanging out near the terracotta elephants of which I am rather fond. They came all the way from a roadside shop in Pune, India, where we lived for a short time for my husband's work. They had travelled unscathed from there to Australia and now were in peril from a cat that appeared to be going bonkers with sheer naughtiness. There was nothing there for her to be chasing with such determination, or so I thought. I removed her from one elephant's back several times, she seemed to think there was something above it that she had a chance of reaching. After a few harsh words from me she appeared to calm down, and thinking she had recovered her sanity I sat down on a chair side on to the elephants.

From the corner of my eye I saw the cat heading back towards one elephant, she was very much in hunting mode. I turned to face her when to my absolute shock I saw what she had been chasing. Wrapped around the corner of the wall near the elephant was what I can only describe as some type of energy being. It appeared to be composed of hexagons ranging in colour from deep navy blue to lighter shades of blue with a sprinkling of hexagons in deep glowing gold. The whole thing had a radiance to it that is difficult to describe, and around the edges there was a slight haze.

Before I could even draw breath it vanished. The cat launched itself onto the elephant's back again and I got up to lift her off. Poor cat, she was convinced that this Being was now hiding behind a print of an elephant that hangs above the terracotta statue. She did not give up until I pulled the print out from the wall and allowed her to see that nothing was hiding there. I think that little Being knew I saw it and decided it was time to depart. Its fun was probably ruined by my moment of extraordinary vision. It left through the print and the wall behind it, that much was made plain by the cat's behaviour.

Now had this event taken place when I was not in the room I strongly suspect my terracotta elephant would be in a similar state as the late Chinese vase, smashed to pieces. I would have put the whole affair down to one of the usual suspects – cat curiosity, boredom, bad behaviour or even spiteful revenge for some perceived slight against cat sovereignty that I had inadvertently performed.

However, I am now in the most excellent position of knowing that there exist little conscious energy Beings that seem to thoroughly enjoy a game of 'tease the cat'. I presume the game could be considered even more entertaining if the cat can be lured into breaking things. Do little energy Beings have a quirky sense of humour then? This would indicate a high level of intelligence.

It seems then, for devoted cat persons who are reading this, there is an altogether fascinating possibility as to the cause behind a cat's sudden weird destructive behaviour. It makes me wonder about the differences between the eyes of the many species on the planet. What other energy beings are going about their daily business just outside the normal range of human vision?

Chapter 2

Tea Drop Teachings

For me, art is a means of mapping. What art I create is simply a symbolic representation of destinations in non-ordinary reality. It is a path back to places of wisdom harvested, sacred spaces in dreams, visions and altered states of consciousness.

Interesting things happened when I was part way through a painting I saw in a dream once. The dream itself was centred on the entwined nature of home, family, friends and life connections. The painting had a very vivid white background and it was of such a striking nature that as I surfaced from the dream I thought to myself, 'I must try and create that.'

It is seemingly a visual representation of many teachings on this planet regarding the interconnectedness of all life. Everywhere one turns now talk is on connections. Science, in terms of quantum physics, is providing evidence of non-local mind and supporting the emerging proposition that consciousness is fundamental, the core reality of being.

Many hours had been gifted to my delivery of a drawing of energy connections, or energy weaving to be exact. The drawing is precise, detailed and intricate. It took weeks. One day I prepared to do more work on this almost complete drawing. The small table that I use was overburdened with a general mishmash of stuff. I had brought a cup of tea to the table. I held the cup in one hand while I shifted things around to make a place on the table for the cup. Suddenly, I became aware that I was holding a full cup of tea precariously above my drawing. A voice within squeaked, 'Oh no, don't spill the tea.' I quickly placed the cup in a cleared space and thought with some relief that I had avoided a catastrophe.

* * *

Unfortunately, this was not so. One tea coloured drip had detached itself from the bottom of the cup where it had been furtively hiding seeking the best moment to test me. On what was originally intended to be a flawless background I now had a brown tea droplet stain.

My brain instructed my body to draw in a deep breath, the prerequisite prelude to a self-derogatory tirade along the lines of: 'You idiot, can't you do anything right, look at it, you ruined it etc.' Yet, while I was still in the act of drawing that breath, my consciousness made me aware of my body. I was astonished to realise that nowhere in my body was there any tension about this situation. It was fascinating, a deep calm was flowing within me. I felt entirely centred and quite serene. The self-shaming abuse never even left the hangar let alone the runway.

Gazing at the offending tea drop mark I noticed what a lovely shape it had formed. My mind started to play with the creative possibilities of the offending stain. I was reminded of a similar experience many years ago. Some children visiting my parent's home had removed and destroyed a stone from the seating edge around a lily pond in the garden. It could not be replaced and the resulting gap was an eyesore. Just after I discovered this vandalism I had an appointment with a very wise old friend and mentor.

I was still hot with outrage as I told her of the damage and how it could not be repaired. She was silent for a moment then looked at me intently and said, "Make a feature out of it." I was entirely taken aback by this fresh perspective. A statue of a dragon was purchased and my husband cemented it into the gap. The pond then had a magical guardian who lent in over the water apparently watching tadpoles playing between the lily pads. It looked beautiful. This had been such a strong teaching that it stayed with me and came to my aid when a tea drop fell.

The question then became what further teaching was to be conveyed by the tea drop episode itself? The drawing had been an illustration of the energy weaving that each of us has in our lives, literally a representation of the multiple strands of connections, our meetings and engagements with others and with life experiences. All of this was taking place within the pristine light of our being, a concept being conveyed by the white backdrop to the drawing. That droplet showed me another perspective – as I incorporated it into the drawing I saw that it was telling me that in essence it is all the one thing. The weave only looks separate from the white backdrop as a result of how we choose a thread of experience from that conscious source then colour the thread, weave it into patterns and make the story of us. The thread beneath the colour and the pattern is at one with the source from which we drew it. As are we.

Previously a voice in a dream had instructed me, stating quite emphatically: "Intelligent beings don't have connections."

My tea drop teaching illustrated that despite appearances to the contrary it is the One life in All life. There is no 'other' to connect to, there is only I AM.

By seeking the positive harvest inherent in the apparent negative experience we can transform our burdens into our blessings. Even the most appalling of events or experiences will always hold within it the wisp of positive, the harvest for our hearts and souls. The appalling becomes a crucible for our expansion into knowing our own oneness with all that is.

May love flow abundantly through the energy weaving of your life.

Chapter 3

The First Giggle

'Total absence of humour renders life impossible'
Colette (1873 – 1954) ...*Chance Acquaintances* 1952.

All my spiritual understandings, my faith, my deep understanding of the eternal gift of life rose up and splattered themselves on the aircraft cabin roof. The elemental forces of the Great Mother were playing a furious game of yo-yo with the plane and I was scared as it brought me face to face with my mortality and the fragility of this life. Turbulence on the long flight home from Los Angeles to Melbourne was the very last thing I needed. As a shamanic apprentice I had just been subjected to several exceedingly long intense days seeped in the mysteries of another aspect of reality and now I desperately needed sleep.

Aeroplanes are hard enough to sleep in without the added joys of bouncing up and down in the sky. In order to circumnavigate the distress and fear I felt and to get some well-deserved rest I began an exercise given to me by Spirit many years ago. It is a practice which assists me to relax or to sleep when disturbing events are taking place.

At that time, life as I had known it was unravelling. As so many people have experienced at one time or another, I would find myself wide awake in the early hours of the morning worrying myself sick over all my problems, not least of which was how to get some sleep. One night as I lay contemplating the misery of me yet again a voice said to me, "What has been the most important event in your life from a positive perspective?" I found myself going back over my life looking at all the great events that had occurred and the next thing I knew it was time to get up. I had slept the rest of the night through. I practiced this night after night and went back to sleep easily and quickly.

Then I reached a point where I was very certain what the single most important event in my life had been, the incredible opportunities that event had gifted me and how that had shaped all of what I consider to be the best of me. After that, if I couldn't sleep, the question changed and has continued to change from time to time. I like to fall asleep thinking about the most amazing event of my life or the happiest memory I have. I find I have so many happy memories that I never run out of them or settle on one and so I sleep. Using this exercise is easy and effective provided the discipline required to pull attention back to the topic in question is applied. Brains try to use crafty circles back to the original negative thoughts that keep one awake and must be trained to the positive path.

On the turbulent journey in question, a voice asked me what the most amazing experience of my life was and I had started thinking of a few such events when it became apparent to me that I was a little bored with this. Instead of continuing I asked Spirit what was the most amazing thing it had ever experienced. I had never previously turned the tables in this exercise. As I asked the question I found myself thinking of all the possible answers that could come from the very Source of Being itself. The Big Bang perhaps, light, the first star, the first cell, the first cell division. There is a huge array of magnificent, amazing occasions that Spirit could call on one would presume. Imagine having all of eternity and infinite space, all pervading consciousness and all of creation in memory and at hand to answer this. How would you decide from so much sheer wonder?

So, my mind was away and racing with infinite possibilities when I heard Divinity speak. It said, "The first giggle." I recall my jaw dropping open, I pulled it back into place and said, "Oh come on, what about the Big Bang or the first star?" "First giggle," shot back at me. I mentioned all the things I could think of, cell division, time, space, but Divinity kept replying, "No, first giggle".

So I tried another tack, I asked what was its happiest memory. "First giggle," it said. Most spectacular event I asked – yes you've guessed it, "First giggle". This continued until Spirit had me giggling a bit myself. I began to get a hint of why this might be such a huge thing in the Mind of Being – humour and the opportunity it offers to see the ridiculous side of the illusions of this reality. The ability to laugh at self can be so freeing.

However, the answer had taken me entirely by surprise and consequently I urged the Almighty most strenuously to reconsider the question and then answer with greater wisdom. After a short time it became apparent that Divinity was quite satisfied with the answer given and no more would be forthcoming. For a brief moment I actually felt a little at fault personally for such a huge failing in the Mind of Being, or perhaps I felt the failure was in my ability to receive the answer clearly. Then I finally accepted that there was much more to this than met the eye, and my curiosity was tweaked.

I commenced a bit of research. Webster's online dictionary definition of giggle surprised me a little. Giggle is considered a foolish or nervous laugh, light, silly or affected. It was linked in several examples to children and young females in particular. The general sense I received was that giggling is considered a feminine form of laughter. Indeed 'gigglers' was slang in the England of 1811 for wanton women. In Norfolk it is referenced as immoderate and senseless laughter. The overall impression I gained from Webster's was that giggling is a female brand of laughter and therefore a frivolous, lesser and meaningless type of levity. When you consider this, what we have is laughter that is not serious, that doesn't appear to have a focus. It isn't manly laughter. I had never before considered laughter to involve aspects of gender in any of its forms of expression. What had begun as a seemingly frivolous answer from Divinity itself now had levels of profundity that required further consideration I decided. After all wasn't God supposed to be a masculine entity? If it considered giggling to be fundamentally amazing, could that assumption of masculinity be incorrect? Is it remotely possible that God should be Goddess? Or as the wise would assume both and, or, neither.

I began to ponder if giggling did indeed have a focus and if that could be the Divinity within us laughing at itself when we giggle. Furthermore, it may be that the very thought of us being separate from It is enough to have It clutching its sides and rendered incoherent with laughter. At some level are we women in on the joke? Is that why it is deemed a feminine laugh, women being more trusting of their wild and intuitive side than men have been encouraged to be. Have we an understanding that when we giggle at 'nothing' we are in fact celebrating simply being and that what is laughing is really our Divine nature?

Rapidly my search parameters expanded to include humour generally. What is the impact of our ability to find humour in, I venture to say, virtually everything on our experience of reality? How does humour serve us? In how many aspects of our lives does it serve us, what is the extent of its range of applications? What is it about humour that it could hold such an esteemed position in the heart of Divinity itself?

I survived the flight home and as the plane landed I jerked awake and heard the Great One say, "Hmmm the First Giggle, good title for a story." I knew I had just been handed a task. Humour is so much a part of life that, unless we are professional comedians, we don't give it much thought. The more I enquired within myself about humour and its role in life the more I realised how little I truly knew about it from a Divine angle. I had long considered humour to be a great survival tool but does it have a prime role or is it entwined throughout all experience? Is that very entwining indicative of its value and importance?

How does one distill the essence of humour or indeed can it be distilled? For me it is a part of the ephemeral fabric of being alive. Many great minds have attempted to pinpoint and corral the crucial factors of humour but, as in our attempts to define the Creator, or creative aspect of cosmic consciousness, we are defeated. However, humour is a major player in life and life is what we are and we are always exploring the depths of our understandings of life and consciousness. I comprehended after that particular plane journey that Divinity itself felt that the correct time had arrived for an exploration of humour from a spiritual perspective.

Did matter itself ride into being on the first bubble of mirth to emerge from the mouth of the heart of the Great Mother of creation? Does a good giggle carry us home to the hearth of that mighty heart for an instant? It's as good a theory as any.

What happens when we laugh?

Fifteen facial muscles contract and there is electrical stimulation of the zygomatic major (cheek muscle) in particular. The epiglottis half-closes, interrupting respiration so that the intake of air becomes irregular and gasping. These behaviours are usually accompanied by noises that can range from sedate giggles to boisterous guffaws.

Source http://people.howstuffworks.com/laughter.htm

Humour and physical health

Research shows that:

· Muscles relax more quickly after watching funny cartoons than after looking at beautiful scenery.

· Laughter reduces some of the hormones associated with the stress response.

· Watching 30 to 60 minutes of comedy results in beneficial changes to the immune system that are still present 12 hours later.

- Humour has been found to reduce pain in some patients.

Laughter is infectious

Humans have a detector in the brain that is specifically devoted to laughter. It responds to laughter by triggering neural circuits that generate more laughter.

Source: McGhee, 1999

Humour and Emotional Health

How does laughter assist emotional health?

Seeing a smile and returning it changes our brain chemistry and gives us a natural high. It is said to give us more pleasure than eating chocolate, shopping, being given money or drinking coffee.

Seems that first giggle set off a chain reaction throughout the material world that is healing, cleansing and reminding us of our sameness.

Chapter 4

Nagged From Beyond The Grave

Let there be no misunderstanding, my late mother-in-law, Joan, and I got on quite well. Yet we were very different people and not often close confidantes. She died in April 2007. I was closer to my father-in-law, Mick, who followed her in July 2009.

Other than when their respective ashes were placed in the ground I did not visit their final resting place. Having been clairaudient all my life I have been able to communicate sometimes with those I love who have entered the next adventure that lies beyond this experience of reality. Mick is a good example of this, we talked fairly often in the months following his death. Not so Joan though. Many times in any given week I would drive past the cemetery where their ashes had been placed side by side, yet I never felt any need to enter the grounds.

One day, more than 12 months after Mick's passing, I had been made late for a psychic development class due to the vagaries of a doctor's appointment. As I approached the cemetery I became aware of a voice telling me to pull the car over and go in. I was in a hurry and didn't want to do this, however the energy of the communication was quite insistent but I knew it wasn't Mick I could feel. Despite the fact that I was running late I parked the car and hurried to the row I knew held the ashes of my late in-laws.

As I approached the long line of brass plaques I saw one had slipped and was hanging on an angle below the line formed by all the others. All was clear I thought, this had to be Mick's plaque. I checked the name on it and sure enough it was his. I turned back towards my car saying to the energy that had brought me here, "Don't worry, I will get this fixed." "No," it shot back, "read it." I turned back, lent down and read the plaque and saw some of the dates on it were incorrect. "Ok," I said, "got it, the plaque will be replaced entirely." By now I had realised I was in touch with Joan – she had always liked things to be neat and tidy and in their place. Mick, in my opinion, wouldn't have given two hoots about the errors on the plaque or its lapsed position. I can only think that he had become tired of Joan's concern about the matter and decided to pass her on to me, telling her I could be reached if necessary. Thanks Mick.

My problem now was that my sister-in-law was their executor and responsible for arranging for the plaque in the first place and hence, responsible for any corrections to be made. She is a good catholic with a sense of humour I appreciate and we get on well. Whilst I am sure she does support the notion of an afterlife, at the time I did feel that her understanding of what that afterlife may be like and my ability to communicate and interact with those in that afterlife may not have been in synchronicity with each other. What to say? I felt she wouldn't have understood her mother contacting me and I didn't feel I could outright lie about why I stopped at the cemetery.

On arriving home later I told my husband, Rod, what had happened and suggested we go to the cemetery the next day and then he could phone his sister and tell her he had been to the cemetery and discovered problems with Mick's plaque. It kept me right out of the picture. A somewhat tortuous path to the truth I admit but coming out of the 'weirdo' closet to my sister-in-law and her husband was not on my agenda at that time. Hence subterfuge, never a good idea.

All went to plan and Rod's sister contacted the cemetery trust to arrange the replacement plaque only to be told that the man in charge of such matters was on a long holiday. Meanwhile, Rod had been offered a job in China and with the problem of the plaque in hand we left for China at the beginning of 2011.

I would like to state here and now to any of the afterlife uninitiated, never, ever, underestimate the nagging power of a spirit no longer confined by physical parameters, such as time or space, and free to ride the waves of boundless consciousness with a concern on its mind.

Over the next five months during the nearly weekly phone conversations Rod had with his sister I was harangued by Joan with, "Ask her about the memorial stone, ask her!" So I would hiss at Rod to ask her about the plaque. He would ask and get the reply that nothing had been done. His sister of course was unaware of any urgency in the matter, after all Mick was dead, what was the hurry? Due to my having not confessed the true nature of things I could hardly pop out with "Your Mum is driving me crazy."

After a few months of this Joan started appearing in my dreams, she would take me to the cemetery and point out the offending plaque. When Rod told his sister that I had dreamt of their Mum and her concerns about the 'memorial stone' as Joan called it, his sister was a bit surprised, but still nothing got done about it. In the end Joan and I reached a truce. I promised if the situation was still not rectified on our return to Australia that we would take care of it ourselves. When we eventually returned home Joan gave me three days grace and then the pressure began again.

A visit to the cemetery showed that nothing had changed in more than six months and I sympathised with Joan's exasperation. Rod went to the cemetery, found the correct person to talk to, arranged and paid for the replacement plaque and we left it in their hands.

Not long after as I was driving past the cemetery I again heard a voice telling me to pull over and go in. I knew from the change of energy in this contact that I would find the matter had finally been dealt with. Sure enough the new plaque, dates corrected, was fixed in line with all the rest. My duty was done.

This experience taught me a few things. One, it is easier to just be the weirdo in the room. Two, that in death as in life we remain individual in our preferences. I had always assumed that the dead would be unconcerned with the state of their final resting place in this realm, that they would have more wonderful experiences to occupy them than such mundane earthly matters, but I was very wrong. Whilst Mick would not have been concerned, I gleaned from Joan that she found it disrespectful, not to mention untidy.

Although we have moved to another area I still have reason to visit the town that they lived in once or twice a year. Now I always call in at the cemetery with small offerings that I think they would like and we have a pleasant time catching up as they seem to be aware of my energy when I am there by their plaques. Joan even lets me know sometimes what she would like me to put there as offerings, small items the purchase of which benefit cancer research. They both had cancer. On one visit Mick suggested, 'You can get me a beer love.' Seriously, after a life time of non-ordinary experiences you would think I would know better but no, I drove to the bottle shop and requested a can of triple X. The man looked at me oddly and then kindly put me straight, "You mean fourX." Not a big drinker me, and definitely not beer. I took that beer to Mick's grave and opened it. I took a swig...Oh My God, it was awesome, like cool nectar. I had a second then a third long swig and then realised that I was being used by my 'hungry ghost' father-in-law. I put the rest down on the ground with him. If beer always tasted like that to him I could see how it had come to play such a large part in his life and consequently the lives of his family. I won't be doing that again. Back to flowers Mick.

Visit those graves, tend them, make offerings, (maybe not alcohol) talk to the departed, such care is appreciated perhaps more than we know.

Chapter 5

Dogs, Books and Mystical Moments

In early 2017 I found myself on the train for a rare visit to my youngest daughter who lives at the other end of our state. It was the first use of my Seniors Card free train trip vouchers. Some time was spent happily congratulating myself on having a body that had reached the grand age of 60 relatively intact. I, of course, am immortal but my personal chariot is showing signs of a little wear and tear, not to mention sag and droop. All in all, at the time though, things were still fairly ship shape.

I looked up from this contemplation of age and its benefits and losses to see my friends Kaye and Nick were also on board. Nick came to sit and chat with me for a while. They were off to a medical appointment in the city. I mentioned that I would have a three-hour stopover in town between trains and that I would use the time to visit the Theosophical Society Bookshop. Nick said he and Kaye did the same when the opportunity arose. We parted company in the city and I walked the several blocks to the bookshop feeling happy to stretch my legs before the next long train ride.

Once there I had soon chosen a few items to buy for my daughter and for a friend before I came across a book I very much wanted to buy for myself. It was called *Mystical Dogs*, written by Jean Houston and was the only copy there. I struggled with myself but decided after long deliberation to be a fiscally responsible adult (very difficult decision for me when faced with books). Reluctantly, I placed the book back on the shelf sending up a silent prayer that it would be there next time when I wasn't buying for others and could indulge myself.

On my return home the following week I attended my weekly meditation class that Nick facilitates. I sat next to Nick for a quick chat while we waited for others to arrive. He informed me that he had bought a wonderful book last week at the Theosophical Society Bookshop, it had practically leapt off the shelf and was the only copy there of *Mystical Dogs* by Jean Houston. Nick said he couldn't put the book down it was so good but when he was finished I could borrow it as he thought I would really appreciate it.

I practically crowed with delight, chuckling that Nick had to buy it for me as I had wanted it so much and the

Universe had made sure that I would get to read it after all.
The words that might be used to describe such an occurrence are:
> Coincidence – a remarkable concurrence of events;
> Synchronicity – simultaneous concurrence of events;
> Connection – state of being connected or linked;
> Telepathy – communication of thoughts by an unknown means or sense;
> Oneness – state of being unified or whole though comprised of two or more parts.

These days I gravitate to Oneness. The state of being one energy or life in all life, a unified being that is constructed of infinite parts all of which contain this conscious flow that of itself knows no boundaries.

It was not correct of me to announce that Nick had to buy the book for me, which could indicate he had no free choice in the matter and was manipulated in some non-ordinary manner. Now I know both Nick and I have a vast depth of interest in all things mystical yet I was surprised that he would buy a book that was about dogs. It had seemed a strange choice to me until he told me that he knew Jean Houston's other books and liked her work.

So, the Universe, being entirely conscious and always with our best interests in its heart and mind, knew both Nick and I would benefit from this book and made sure

Nick found it after I had decided I couldn't justify the cost at the time. The choice to buy the book was always as free for Nick as it had been for me. Interesting that when something is meant to occur then it has multiple means of doing so.

Now I fully comprehend that this is not an earth-shattering tale of the paranormal by any standards. In fact, I would be greatly surprised if something similar had not occurred once or twice in the lives of most people reading this. Such small events happen and we marvel for a moment then move on, relegating them to a minor memory of something a bit out of the ordinary. The real question is why does the apparently inexplicable become an event we don't choose to focus upon? An occurrence which, though welcome, we remain wary of and which we don't wish to examine closely and marvel at for too long. We do tend to hide these magic moments and whisper them only, if at all, to a few we think we can trust not to laugh at us. Why don't we celebrate and honour the non-ordinary wonders more?

Science, in the main, still denies any causal connectivity in such events, and the accepted world view remains that they are simply unconnected blips in the normal world that only silly people attach significance to. We fear appearing foolish by honouring the as yet unexplained, not inexplicable, magic in the world. Who cares to be burnt by ridicule? No one. Yet to strengthen anything it must be used, practised, studied, given attention, treated with excitement and curiosity, explored in all its stages and states.

If we take to our hearts the tiny 'blips' in our lives we begin to comprehend their significance as a continuous worldwide stream of signposts all pointing to one thing – that consciousness is at the very core of existence. Awareness permeates all matter and can, harnessed to wisdom, manufacture delights and miracles as yet undreamed of.

As I contemplated writing this account of the non-ordinary, lying across most of the couch and my knees was my very own mystical mountain of a dog. I will take this opportunity to relate his arrival into our lives as a further example of the wonders we are still frightened to shine our inner, let alone outer, lights upon.

We had a man working with us on a house we were completing and this man had a dog very similar in appearance to a golden retriever. Her name was Nancy. One night I had a dream that Nancy was running across our yard being closely followed by another dog. When next I saw him I told our friend I thought he would be getting another dog soon as I had this dream of Nancy with a young dog.

Not long after my daughter called to tell me of puppies available in a nearby town. I had always wanted an irish wolfhound or an english mastiff and these pups were a cross of both breeds. We went…just to look…yes, well Walter came home with me. He and the runt were the only two pups remaining from a large litter. I think he was still there because his eyes were blue. Within a day or two of coming home with me his eyes started to change to a light golden colour. I like to think the blue eyes made sure Walter was there waiting for me.

A few months later I looked across the yard and saw the exact scene from my dream, Walter, a young gangly dog running behind Nancy. The dream came true precisely, the only error had lain in my interpretation. I finally had my mountain of a dog who rarely leaves my side. I hesitate to tell of the damage a 70-plus kilo dog can do to polished wooden floors but the good he does in my heart far outweighs it (no pun intended).

I like to stop to think of the potential inherent in my dreams on a daily basis, and they respond quite dramatically to this attention and are powerful tools of instruction, advice and gifts beyond measure.

For those among you who are lovers of animals, dogs in this case, and like nothing better than to delve with abandon into mysticism then I can highly recommend *Mystical Dogs* by Jean Houston.

Chapter 6

Shamans, Dogs and The Afterlife

Names have been changed in this tale.

There exists a photo of my friend Ann, taken in June 2011 when we were both attending a shamanic event in New Mexico. It was the first year of a four year shamanic apprenticeship. Ann had just been telling a group of us about the death of her beloved dog. When I took the photo I actually saw the super bright flash of light though the viewfinder. This had never happened to me before. I had taken quite a few orb photographs but I had never previously seen the energy itself. Instantly I knew I had caught the spirit of her recently deceased dog. The energy had shot through from the back seat and bounced up and down and all around the front seat. Just like a dog greeting its owner. If you look carefully you can see the energy trail, no speck of dust this. It made me really happy to have caught such doggy enthusiasm on my camera. The joy in the energy was palpable.

Fast forward to early 2019. A shaman friend was nearly ready to transition. Penny was one of those charismatic people who drew others to her with ease. Although our abodes were far apart, she in Miami, Florida and myself in Australia, I never lost touch with Penny, I loved and admired her. Penny was the epitome of a powerful shaman, full of love and light and healing to all who knew her. She was also the very closest of friends to Ann who was with Penny and her family throughout the long drawn out process of her illness and death. Ann was there for the hospice time and there for the transition. Penny was still in her 50s and so many of us were saddened by what we perceived as her early passing. One person summed it up by saying that Penny had taught them how to live and then taught them how to die. That is a shaman.

As I had discovered early in the year that I had major health issues myself, Penny and I had talked a bit via Messenger. Belonging to a tribe of amazing shamans all over the world and knowing full well the power of prayer, or focused intent if you prefer, I had sent out a call to everyone I could think of to pray for me and to send love and healing energy my way. Penny saw this request and that is when we began to chat.

Just a few days before her passing Penny and I were talking in the middle of the night, she awake with a body that was freezing cold and me awake with chemo induced insomnia. She told me her body was all 'butterfly gooey". I thought it an apt description of the approaching event. The first time I had ever seen her she had been wearing a top that was designed with a huge painting of a butterfly on the back. It was stunning, as was she. Butterflies at the beginning and the end seemed appropriate for our friendship.

Only days after her death I had a marvellous dream of Penny. She was younger and bursting with wellbeing, her hair long and blonde again. She told me that where she was now there was no lack, want or going without for anybody. We hugged and I told her I loved her. There was a dog with her, a black labrador with a name starting with B. When I woke I wrote the dream down. It had been a powerful dream and I shared it with another friend of Penny's who encouraged me to share this with Penny's family.

I bought a card and proceeded to write down the dream as well as a few other bits and pieces. One was something that had come to me on a walk a few weeks prior that I had shared with Penny:

> Perhaps death is a spontaneous remission
> transforming the illusions of matter
> into the Truth of Life.

Whilst writing the dream I heard a voice telling me to put in the bit about the dog being with her. I questioned the voice, saying Penny didn't have such a dog. I was reminded that it is just such small and apparently trivial or meaningless pieces of information that can be of great importance in assisting others to see that life continues past the boundary of bodily death. Dutifully I popped in the bit about the black Labrador with a B name and sent the card off in the mail.

A couple of days before the card arrived at its destination both Ann and Penny's husband had dreams that were similar to mine, Penny was young and vibrant. The day before the card arrived Ann had come across my request on Messenger for prayers and had seen Penny's response which talked of the courage required to ask for help. When the card arrived Penny's husband took the envelope to Ann and asked her to read the card to him. She said she was shocked to see it had come from Australia and had my name on it just after she had been drawn to my post.

Ann said that she cried a little as she read and then she got to the part about the dog and began to cry so much she couldn't keep reading for a while. She couldn't believe what she was reading. The black Labrador whose name started with B was her 15-year-old dog Bailee who had been put to sleep around December, not long before Penny died. Ann kept a photo of Penny right next to a photo of Bailee on her altar. Ann told me that it meant everything to her that I had sent this information from my dream. She said she has only ever had two dogs and both managed to contact me after they had died.

Trust a shaman woman as strong as Penny to put all this together so meticulously – the power of dreams to heal us in a multitude of ways is simply amazing. The power of the 'dead' (Dreamer Entering Another Dimension) to reach through the veil and lovingly touch and mend us is humbling.

* * *

When I was a little girl all I really wanted to be was a veterinarian. Although this vocation remains unfulfilled, the Universe has compensated somewhat as so many of my other worldly experiences seem to involve dogs. Pet loving people can be inclined to worry about whether their pets have souls and if they survive death and go to heaven. Religions don't seem to respond well to these concerns, some New Age thinkers will advise that animals have a group soul and lose their individuality upon death. A few say that if we love the animal deeply this will guarantee their continuation in individual form. All are just theories and we would do well to remember this, particularly in light of some of the true tales mentioned here.

Ectoplasm always seemed to me to be the biggest load of bunkum out there, old photos of mediums exuding what looked like cheesecloth didn't encourage me to believe in the stuff. It was only when I saw it with my own eyes that my understanding of its authenticity grew. Both times I have seen ectoplasm it has been in full light. The second time I saw ectoplasm was at the beginning of 2007. We were renting a house in rural Victoria and weren't able to have a dog on the premises. Our eldest daughter was taking care of our dog for us but I missed having a dog around. Dogs are master teachers of unconditional love and of the true nature of love. On my daily walks I could frequently hear the jingling sound of dog registration tags behind me, sometimes so clearly that I would turn around expecting to see a dog but there was never one present. I could occasionally hear the actual footsteps of a dog too. Even in my dream life I was being brought dead dogs that needed guidance and care.

One morning as we were about to go shopping I opened the car door and a few long ribbons of translucent white material floated out the door. My understanding that this was a living thing was so instantaneous and complete that without thought I stepped back opening the door wider and said out loud, "Sorry, excuse me." The material drifted out and past me and then disappeared. I was musing on this and telling my husband about it as I climbed into the car and started to drive out of the garage. Suddenly, my husband said, "What's that smell?" I sniffed and then smiled happily and told him that it was dog soap he could smell. He agreed as it was a distinctive smell from both our childhoods of a very well-known brand of dog soap that both our mothers had used when bathing the family dogs. We concurred that a deceased dog had been in the car and it was good that ghostly wet dogs don't leave sopping car seats!

* * *

To conclude this chapter I will share a personal favourite experience of mine involving a 'dead' dog.

We had purchased a house in Monbulk in the hills outside Melbourne. It was a bank repossession and in a very sorry state as the previous owner had pulled out fittings from the house and done a lot of damage. At one end of the house was a huge fernery which had once housed an extremely large spa bath. My husband and I were faced with a room that had a small swimming pool sized hole in the floor. We covered it over and then built a raised dais over the area on which we then placed our waterbed. The room made a beautiful bedroom.

Once our bed was in place it wasn't long before I began to notice something a little odd was taking place. My youngest child was a very light sleeper who woke several times every night, hence I was always on alert for her call. What began to form was a pattern where at the same time every night I would be woken by the sound of running footsteps coming up the tiled centre passageway of the house towards our bed. I would immediately be wide awake only to realise that there was no one there.

A few other odd things started to occur. It became apparent that some sort of energy was being attracted to our youngest girl. Once when I was changing her nappy she pointed to her favourite toy which was placed on a high shelf in her bedroom. It was a musical toy and she very obviously wanted to hear it. There was a clicking sound then the toy began to play all on its own. Although this was quite creepy I knew that whatever was around liked her and meant no harm. On another occasion we had been out at night and returned very late for us – due to my tiredness from being woken several times a night we rarely ventured out in the evening. When we went into the baby's bedroom to put her to bed a light flew into the room and went round and round the room at high speed. Both my husband and I could see this light and I telepathically picked up some frantic thoughts along the line of; 'Where have you been, is she alright?'

All of this was taking place in conjunction with my starting to attend a spiritualist church and beginning to meditate regularly. After some months a change occurred one night. Instead of stopping when I woke up the footsteps continued right up to my side of the bed and I could clearly hear something panting in my right ear. For a brief moment I was absolutely terrified and then a voice told me that what was present was a dog, it was a wet dog and it wanted to shake water over me as dogs like to do for a bit of entertainment. I realised that indeed the energy and the panting were very doggy in nature.

Then I made a mistake. In my mind I talked to the dog and told it this was my house now and it had to leave. I heard it turn around and walk all the way to the other end of the house and then for the first time ever I heard it leave the house. At that moment I realised I hadn't told it where to go or what to do, I had just vanquished it. I had rejected something quite harmless that simply wanted to interact with our family. I blamed the vestiges of the fear I had initially felt for my unthinking response. I felt very guilty and sad.

The dog never woke me again but I felt concern for it. I knew it had drowned in the spa where the bed now stood on its dais. Perhaps it came to that spot every night at the same time that it had died there. My intuition told me though that I hadn't completely solved the ghost dog problem, he was still outside and around the house. Eventually, we moved away for work and rented the house out. The tenants loved the place and wanted to buy it and we decided to sell to them. I returned to the property to collect some things that weren't part of the sale and for some reason I felt compelled to tell the new owners about my ghostly friend. As I finished telling them their eyes swung around to each other. I was thinking that they probably thought I was insane when one of them said that the other one had been experiencing a repetitive dream of a dog drowning! They had become so concerned about this dream that they were about to securely cover the spring, which was the water supply for the property, as they had thought the dream was a warning that one of their dogs was going to drown.

It was reassuring to know that my intuition was correct – the ghost dog was still around. I hadn't sent it into some horrible limbo existence. Furthermore, it was validating – other people could, and had, sensed what I could sense.

My interactions with this ghost were very strong. When I have my own moments of doubt about life after death, or even about my own sanity, I think back to this poor drowned dog and know that if a dog's consciousness can survive death so effectively – that it can not only communicate its survival but form new bonds – what more could we humans be capable of?

This experience illustrates that animals are composed of life energy, or consciousness, that is the same as in all living things. This energy or consciousness continues on eternally and very obviously in an individual form. If we stop looking at the differences in life forms and comprehend the underlying consciousness as the one creative principle in all then we step into new frontiers of exploration into life itself. This core of oneness offers infinite diversity and potentialities.

Of course, for many of us the most important result of this experience, this tiny transformational tale, is that all dogs eventually go to heaven, they survive, they thrive. They don't merge into a group soul and they aren't saved from such a horrid end so much by being loved as by being love. Their own inherent nature is the same life, the same loving consciousness that we all share.

Chapter 7

Huntsman Spider Message

This may not appear at first to be a story concerned with consciousness but stick with it to a very surprising ending.

Huntsman spiders, those hairy eight-legged house and car companions have been the bane of my life. My earliest memory is of a particularly splendid huntsman on a pink wall directly in front of me. The vision is accompanied by a soundtrack of my older sister's scream fading into the distance as she ran away from this large, almost meaty, visitor. I was 18 months old and at that moment I decided this strange creature must be something to be deeply feared.

Since that introduction I have encountered far more than my fair share of these fast moving horrors. Most

Australians have one or two good huntsman stories to tell, I have so many I could write a book. I will attempt to summarise them for you:

Numerous curtain and blind moments, they love hiding in such places.

Letter boxes, oh my word, more times than I can count the letters have come out with spider attachments.

Countless 'behind the picture on the wall' events, with long hairy legs waggling enticingly at me. Inside cupboards and between books on a shelf. Under the flap of a saddle, that was a close call as I used to hold the flap up with my head while doing up the girth.

One fell on my chest in bed when I opened the book from the bedside table in which it had tucked itself away for a spider snooze.

Out of the mouth of a little used garden tap, as I turned the water on it hastily emerged and climbed to higher ground...my hand.

Out of the inner workings of my electric typewriter at work, showing my age here. I was rescued by a greatly amused male client and just as well as I may have never typed again if it had escaped back into the depths from which it had emerged.

So many in car doors that I have lost count. Quite a few windscreen visits. The mandatory sun visor moment in the car. I have even pulled out the car seat belt only to be greeted by a huntsman riding it like some fairground adventure for daring arachnids.

There was the hatching of hundreds of the little blighters, though to be fair, at the size of a little finger nail they were almost cute. An entire wall was covered with miniature monsters all scuttling into cracks and crevices in order to grow and then leap out as mature brutes.

There is the classic insurance advertisement moment of one on my bare foot whilst I was driving the car. I have large, broad feet. This guy not only straddled my foot his legs went over the sides and he held on despite frantic attempts to brush him off using my other foot. By the time I looked up I had crossed over the other side of the road and was headed for a large tree. I pulled up and began the quest to find the passenger who had gone into hiding. I knew I had to find him or I would never, ever, drive that car again.

My husband, children and I moved to an area in the countryside of Victoria that I now believe to be the ancestral home of all huntsman spiders. I discovered six huge ones on our first day there, all of them in the kitchen cupboards. I seriously considered selling the place or at least abstaining from cooking for the foreseeable future.

There was the one that had my youngest daughter screaming at me over the sound of the chainsaw whilst collecting firewood. It was halfway up my back and making, God forbid, for my head. Let's not even discuss the ones of all sizes in the firewood I had to collect, split and carry into the house for years.

This dear old country house was full of the damn things, another classic, under the toilet seat. One shot out on the toilet paper when I pulled on the roll. A stifling summer night, sleeping naked and uncovered – yes, it fell off the ceiling and ran up my leg. I think I may have actually levitated on that occasion.

Making a refreshing cup of tea I boil the kettle, make and drink a cup of tea. A little later decide to have a second cup, still enough water in the kettle but this time when I pour the water into my cup it comes with the added bonus of well stewed huntsman.

I'm sure by now you are getting the picture of my lifetime of hauntings by huntsman spiders. There are of course shamanic aspects of these frequent visitations, such as the perspective of what this spider energy might be trying to gift me. Or that I am being assisted to face and conquer a large fear. Still, something much more intriguing than these lessons came about through my fear of these spiders.

This occurred in 2013. I was off to bed and did my usual careful check of the ceiling and corners for huntsman. While I was no longer a total wreck if I came across one – decades of hairy multi-legged inundations had desensitised me to some degree. I still had a deep horror of having one on my head or even worse, my face. Reassured on this occasion that all was well I hopped into my comfy bed and very quickly dropped off to sleep lying on my back. I was woken within a short time by what literally felt like an energetic kick of great magnitude to my solar plexus, a huge surge of energy that shot through me. My eyes flew open. Immediately, I was aware of a large huntsman on the ceiling directly above my head. I didn't move a muscle, which was incredible considering I had a history of lightning speed reactions when it came to huntsman evasion.

Picture it, my idea of true horror, a huntsman on my face and a large member of the species on the ceiling directly above my head and I don't move. Furthermore, I stop looking at it. Why? Simple, something else was happening on that ceiling and it was amazing. A circular section of the ceiling about 20cm in diameter was no longer solid. It was moving, fluid, rotating and shimmering slightly. Then it suddenly snapped back to a solid ceiling as though a door had shut. That is when I recalled the spider and leapt out of bed calling my long-suffering husband to do the deed of spider removal yet again.

This experience illustrates how closely we are held in an infinite embrace, deeply loved and cared for by a consciousness that exists in all dimensions and knows no barriers. How powerful is that consciousness, all aspects of it, our loved ones, guides and contacts? Matter itself can be manipulated and even dissolved in order to assist us. It brings into question the nature of this reality. Is it as solid as it appears or is that apparent cohesion of matter just an agreed upon perception? Quantum physics suggests this to be so. We are composed more of void or space than of solid. The ancient wisdom of the Heart Sutra is recalled: Void is Form and Form is Void. It seems that consciousness pervades all, we live within it and our wellbeing is of paramount importance to that cherishing intelligence.

This is how one of my greatest fears became the conduit for a journey to a vastly broadened appreciation of what it means to be loved beyond all measure, cherished, conscious and eternally an aspect of the web of being. What a blessed life I lead.

Chapter 8

Hearing Voices, Rasputin and Fish

In 2013 I came across a very interesting book written by a woman about her communications with her brother after he had died. He began communicating with his grieving sister a few weeks after his death and his sister wrote a book about the things he told her, in particular about what happens after we die. However, in addition to comments about the afterlife the brother also suggested remedies for people who had health issues. I recall one was a recommendation for green tea consumption and in a couple of instances he suggested Bach Flower remedies for people.

Just after finishing the book I went on my customary morning walk, which has transformed over time to a state of moving meditation. I was pondering the communications in the book and in particular the health advice. This was of interest as I suffered a chronic mild illness with dietary and fatigue associations. I was 'in the zone' as I shot a question the brother's way. "Okay, what would you prescribe for me?" I asked. Even though I am clairaudient I wasn't that sure of receiving an answer. However, if such an answer did occur I fully expected to hear of a Bach Flower remedy that might help my condition.

Hardly had I mentally asked before a voice replied, "Rasputin's concoction". This brought me to a halt and my mouth may well have hung open, not wise during spring in the High Country where flies abound. Rasputin was a Siberian peasant, mystic and self-proclaimed holy man. From late 1906 he acted as healer to the Tsar's son and heir, Alexei, who suffered from haemophilia. He became a powerful influence in the court of Tsar Nicholas. Rasputin was assassinated in 1916 by a group of conservative noblemen who opposed his influence over the Tsarina Alexandra and the Tsar. It has been suggested that the British Secret Service, at the very least, knew of the plot to kill Rasputin and approved as his removal kept Russia at war with Germany. Rasputin it is thought, had been urging the Tsar to negotiate with Germany for peace between Germany and Russia. Rasputin was a very colourful character.

Whilst all this was very interesting, what on earth was Rasputin's concoction? Certainly not something I had ever heard of before. Intrigued, as soon as I arrived back home I went straight to the computer with its frustratingly slow internet connection and googled. Given Rasputin's reputation for being somewhat odd I did wonder if I would find something involving ingredients like eye of newt. To my extreme surprise, relief and gratification however I was presented with this:

RASPUTIN'S CONCOCTION:
2 small cod approx. 1kg in total
1 cup milk and 1 cup thick cream
3cm of grated fresh ginger, 1 tablespoon paprika,
salt and freshly ground black pepper.

Method:

Clean fish, cut fillets into small pieces and place in saucepan with the ginger, cream, paprika and milk. Bring to scalding point. When bubbles appear at the edges of the pan simmer for about 10 minutes or until fish is done. Don't boil. Season with salt and pepper to taste.

* * *

According to Maria, Rasputin's daughter, this was his favourite dish. In Petrograd and Moscow restaurants would have it prepared if they expected Rasputin to dine. He himself attributed his vigour and virility to this dish.

It is with great sadness that I report I was unable to procure fresh cod locally. The fishmonger informed me it gets sent overseas and all we have here is smoked cod. I did try the recipe with smoked cod but it was too salty for me and thus I have never consumed the soup on any regular basis. Hence I cannot testify to is efficacy with regard to treating my health issues. Ginger has powerful anti-inflammatory and anti-oxidant properties and also soothes the intestinal tract. Cod is high in B12, B6 and niacin and contains omega-3 with anti-inflammatory associations. Knowing all this and how much my body adores ginger I strongly suspect that the brother's recommendation was entirely appropriate for me. Should I ever have the good (perhaps not the correct word) fortune of finding myself living in proximity of a fish market I shall of course do the obvious.

This is a fabulous experience because it is so out of left field – I mean seriously, how many people have ever heard of Rasputin's Concoction, let alone know what it is? Obviously once again consciousness is just champing at the bit to alert me of its omnipresence and omniscience. The fact is that every piece of information is readily available if we know how to ask for it. I love that my receiving a reply from presumably the 'dead' brother from the book was an immediate occurrence. His consciousness and mine were able to communicate through the cosmic consciousness of which we are both an aspect, without any of the time and space complications we endure in the material world.

Life is so expanded by enjoying the understanding that the fewer barriers I have in place to experiencing universal wisdom the more miraculous life itself becomes. There we have it, hearing voices, Rasputin and fish soup all tied up into one more fabulous experience and demonstration of consciousness not being bound to a body.

Chapter 9

What's In A Name?

It is true, I must admit, that I had become a little addicted to the detective series from Switzerland airing on Netflix – *Der Bestatter*, (*The Undertaker*). I was up to the final series available and a few episodes into it when something amazing happened.

In the episode concerned a Japanese man is murdered and his funeral is arranged according to Japanese Buddhist principles. A detail of this ceremony is paying a Buddhist monk to give the deceased a Kaimyo name. This is a name designed to prevent the return of the deceased if someone remaining here calls their name. A ghost prevention technique.

Apparently the longer the Kaimyo name the better and it tends to lengthen in direct proportion to the size of the fee paid to the monk. Nothing like religions for making money out of people when at their most vulnerable or guilty.

However, watching this, I was rather enchanted by the concept of being given a name at the time of death as we do at the beginning of life. An acknowledgement perhaps that the dead still retain consciousness and are moving into a new reality and expression of their being. I started the very obvious question in my mind: 'I wonder what my Kaimyo...' I didn't even complete the question in my mind before I heard the reply, "Breath of Heaven Passing Through."

I was overwhelmed and my eyes filled with tears of happiness. It was, and is, the most sublimely beautiful name I have ever heard, and it is my name. I repeated it several times to myself and every time I said it a rush of energetic delight flowed through every cell in my body.

The next day I did a bit of research on Kaimyo names in Wikipedia and other sources, all of which upheld the definition I had gleaned from The Undertaker episode. Yet I felt compelled to keep looking and these days I tend to listen to my intuition. I finally came across a glossary of Zen Buddhist terms that was more comprehensive. It said, apart from what I already knew, a Kaimyo, (or Dharma) name is given during a Jukai ceremony, an initiation into Buddhism, making one a member of Buddha's family. It is often a unique buddhist name which may at times express certain qualities the Master has observed in his or her disciple.

Then the old doubts and self-criticism moved in: I don't deserve a name like this, I am not worthy; I kill spiders and mosquitos and flies, although I do emulate my mother and put flies out the door if I can catch them. Anyway, not worthy, undeserving, heaps better people than me on the planet who would be deserving of such a brilliant shining name.

Then it hit me, we all deserve and share this name, it gathers us beneath the banner of compassion. It is the core of our Being. Breath of Heaven Passing Through is what every single one of us truly is, a breath of that wondrous creative heart and mind of pure being from which we spring forth to hover for an infinitesimal beat before we are inhaled back into bliss.

We are Heaven's breath passing through this dimension. To the extent that we know and live our Oneness of Being lies the measure of our ability to make that bliss, that is our truth, manifest here, now.

Chapter 10

Feathers, Feathers Everywhere

I am unaware of when it was that I first came to understand that a crow's feather would come my way to indicate I was on the right path in a spiritual sense. Sometimes other feathers appear in strange places as if by magic in response to a question I have posed to the Cosmic Consciousness but most often it will be a crow feather. I could go further and tell that I have had a few encounters with the birds themselves which, had they occurred and been observed in days long gone by, would have most definitely seen me burnt to a crisp.

Crows are the stuff of myth and magic in cultural beliefs across the globe. They are thought to symbolise various aspects of knowing and creation, balance, spiritual law, intuitive knowledge, release from past beliefs, skill and cunning. Crows are also sometimes seen as psychopomps, accompanying souls to the new life after this mortal life ends. They are known to be very clever and adaptable and able to survive in almost any situation. The God Odin kept two crows as messengers and Apollo is said to have turned all crows black from their original white in a fit of anger.

There is a strong affinity for crows that has rippled through me all my life. Their strange calls and talk thrill me and ignite my curiosity. I hear one as I write and also note two crows are depicted on the clothes I am wearing. A painting of one hangs behind me on the wall above my altar.

My father didn't approve of crows or my fascination with them, he condemned them for being carrion eaters. Yet imagine how much smellier and generally unpleasant the world would be if some valiant creatures didn't consume that which is offensive to us. They do us a great service in this respect.

It was both normal and required in my birth family that one was at all times obedient to my father's wishes. Hence, I didn't wear green, (enough photosynthesis in the world), yellow (the colour of fear) or purple (indicative of royalty on which Dad frowned.) Already I can sense your concern for my mental and emotional well-being which I hasten to assure is perfectly fine in all, or most, areas. Despite Dad being the One Authority I never did surrender my love of crows to the bonfire of his tyranny. It stayed undiscovered by paternal forces safely swimming in the sacred river's flow of my soul.

Later in life, during the decision-making process of whether or not to undertake a shamanic apprenticeship, I steadfastly resisted shamanism and my spirit guides insistence that I should study it. I had spent years following the understandings of Murdo MacDonald-Bayne. He taught that one does not need a guru, priest or authority between the self and the divine, and that ritual and dogma were unnecessary tools and detrimental to the quest for the divine. Shamanism seemed to me a step backwards in my spiritual life, it appeared to encompass a great deal of ceremony and ritual and the use of 'tools' to reach spirits and guidance.

I fought the pressure to take up that apprenticeship with a depth of stubbornness that only a fellow Taurean could comprehend. One day on a walk as I was telling spirit once again that I couldn't see a point in going in the direction of shamanism, I became aware of crow feathers on the ground. There was no crow corpse, simply a multitude of feathers – they literally began to rain down on me and were everywhere over the several blocks that I walked. I couldn't ignore such a magnificent abundance of crow energy and having got the hint I started the apprenticeship, yet my resistance remained. At that time I continuously questioned this aspect of my spiritual journey.

Within the first six months of my apprenticeship we moved to China during their winter. The snow was falling in gentle swirls outside the hotel window where we were to stay until a suitable apartment was located. I was full of doubts and questions. It occurred to me to ask spirit to send me a feather if I was on the correct path, yet a further reassurance for this doubting Thomasina.

I had barely formulated the request when a voice gently reprimanded me: 'It's winter, there is snow, the birds all need their feathers now.' Feeling a very self-centred and chastened apprentice I applied myself to the work. Fortunately, not long after this I had a dream where I talked with Murdo MacDonald-Bayne and he helped me understand why I had to learn that I didn't need tools and ceremony before I undertook this apprenticeship. It was simply so I would use them correctly and never hand my power to them, remembering at all times that I could go directly to the divine source if needed. This instruction allowed me to proceed with confidence upon the shamanic path.

It was a year or two later, long after our return to Australia, that once again I experienced some reservations about my spiritual direction. I asked spirit to send me a feather if all was as it was meant to be. I glanced out the window onto a cold and dreary grey vista, recalling immediately that once again it was winter and the birds would need their feathers. Apologies were swiftly sent to the Universe and my feathered brethren for my thoughtless request and I forgot all about it.

The next day my youngest daughter asked me what she should do with some books she no longer wanted. I suggested we take them to the local second-hand bookshop, the largest shop of its kind I have come across. It is full to bursting with row upon row of shelves crammed with books written on every conceivable subject. It was drizzling with rain as we carted her boxes of books into the shop. I left her to chat with the shop owner and began to peruse the book treats on offer. After a few minutes my eyes lit upon a book on a shelf above my head. It was about Rosslyn Chapel in Scotland and I thought it would be something one of my cousins would enjoy. I lifted it down and opened it at random to find a long black crow feather in excellent condition. It had been used as a bookmark. Given that the book reeked of cigarette smoke I imagine the feather was as relieved as I was amazed at its release from the book.

Though not of a religious background, the Bible phrase, '...not a single sparrow can fall to the ground without your Father knowing it' leapt to mind. It was apparent that not even a single feather can be placed in a book without the Universe knowing it. I had asked for a feather and it had appeared, even in winter. Can this really be shrugged off as simply coincidence? What is it that could know, not only of my request for a feather, but of a lesson well learnt not to ask for things from others that they still need themselves and the whereabouts of a beautiful crow feather trapped in a smelly book? Is Cosmic Consciousness as precise and all-knowing as this scenario indicates? Can our mortal lives be this accurately choreographed? Interesting that some believe crows also encourage people to explore new vistas and perceptions, look beyond the normal range.

In 2013 I was given a blessing poem by a spirit guide:

> Blessings blessings everywhere
> let them fill the Holy air
> that there shall be no space to spare
> that is not filled with blessings fair.

I asked what was meant by the term holy air as I knew it did not refer to just the air we breathe. The guide replied that it was the name of the void within all matter. It is what we call the space in atomic structure through which flows the Cosmic Consciousness that orchestrates all that is. It is not subject to space or time or the laws of matter – which it creates. It is entirely seamless and fundamental to all existence. Thus, what happens at one point is instantaneously known at all points. In fact there are no points in this reality, just Presence, being itself, all aware. Hence the finding of a feather upon request, lodged in a book, in winter, at that time of year when birds need their feathers. Consciousness knows where the feather is, knows I have a 'belief' that a feather can be an indication of a correct path spiritually and allows the two aspects of its own Being to greet each other.

Simple really, yet awe inspiring in its completeness and the implications implicit in that conscious Oneness. The unity of it is magnificent and not attained at the cost of individuality which resides within the Oneness.

Chapter 11

There is a Snake in My Marriage Basket

Part of my shamanic apprenticeship involved the construction of a marriage basket. Such a basket represents many things – the balanced male and female aspects of self in unity. The Navajo view these baskets sometimes as maps through which they chart their lives, it can be a receptacle for their blue corn wedding cakes. Their baskets have a gate for spirit to come and go and can also be used as powerful healing tools. They can represent the womb from which all things are birthed. Marriage baskets and their meanings and use is an involved study.

My marriage basket was due for completion by late 2013. On July 26 2013 I dreamt I was at the completion ceremony. There was a snake wrapped around the rim of my marriage basket. On waking I thought to myself that a snake in the basket might be a little difficult to manage in this reality. On July 28 I had another dream wherein my deceased sister tells me she knows the meaning of the name Kim. I tell her it means noble leader. She replies that she has a book that says it means one who is able to lift or raise people from below (state of enclosed consciousness) using the power of the Nagual. To have such a powerful mythical creature as an ally to assist me in helping people expand their perceptions of being seemed a little overawing. I found myself quite subdued over the next few days as I contemplated the nature of the message in this dream and more importantly the nature of Nagual.

My research on the Nagual told me that Carlos Casteneda, an American author who wrote a series of books describing his shamanism training, thought it describes a person who is able to lead people to new areas of perception. Other definitions online told different stories: a Nagual is the benefactor of an apprentice, a guide to freedom, representative of a human who realises their Divine self, the recovery of the unity of our two sides both tonal and Nagual as the secret promise of the feathered serpent, the Aztec Quetzalcoatl.

There were more understandings and it seems that no one truly knows what Nagual is only that it is, and its powers are many. For me the standout understanding was the reptilian nature of the Nagual, the recovery of self-unity and that it can be an ally to an apprentice. These concepts were in line with my marriage basket dream and the subsequent creation of the basket and with my shamanic path to Being.

Following such powerful and instructive dreams I returned to my waking life problem: just how does one place a snake in a marriage basket in this day and age?

Off I trotted like an obedient little shaman to the modern-day hunting ground called the shops and procured a rubber snake. After much difficulty I attached it in a tenuous and haphazard manner to the rim of my basket. The result was that it looked appalling and the energy it created was dreadful. I removed the offending replica. What to do now?

At the time we lived in the country and a beautiful river bordered our land. Snakes were regularly spotted along the banks, on the roads, in the garden and on one occasion trying to come under the front door. In spring some years earlier I had come across a snake skin which had been shed.

Well, it's not long until spring I thought, I will find a skin and put it in the basket. Easy! I waited until the end of the first week of spring but no snake skin appeared serendipitously anywhere in my surrounds. I knew that my guides were not going to let me down but the ceremony was rapidly approaching and I was a little tense about procuring my snake energy for the basket. I enlisted my husband Rod's assistance in the quest telling him I needed a snake for my marriage basket and to keep his eyes open for a snake skin please.

On the 9th of September I had another dream of a huge sea serpent submerging – things were ramping up. Later that day we returned from shopping and I let Rod out at the top of our long driveway to open and close the property gate. I left him at the gate to walk down to the house as usual and drove down to begin unloading the groceries. As he walked to me on the verandah he said, "Hold out your hand." He often brought me frogs in this manner and fully expecting a frog I held out my hand and he dropped a dead, dried baby snake onto my palm. I had my promised snake for the marriage basket.

As the basket was about balance and unity of my male and female aspects, I particularly appreciate the delicacy of the actual event. As the female partner of a marriage I had dreamt of the requirement of a snake and applied feminine wisdom in the form of intuition and faith to know it was possible and to wait upon that and to ask my male life partner to do what men do, go out into the world and hunt down the goods. Unity of male and female powers had located the snake energy required.

The Universe is simply amazing isn't it? Never think that your wants or needs are beyond your ability to achieve. There is no order of difficulty in miracles, they are simply the result of a moment's perfection in answer to our call. Cosmic Consciousness is always waiting for our return to it as the only true source of love and abundance.

One way I use the power of the Nagual is by sharing my non-ordinary life experiences as a means of demonstrating the possibilities available to every human being in their lives. A simple shift of perception, the sidelining of a belief can be all it takes to totally alter life circumstances and open our hearts to the wonder of Being. The accounts of my non-ordinary life experiences are all about the depth of love, beauty and possibilities that swirl around all of us and are available to all. There is an intelligence so vast moving behind and through all that happens that it can plan and arrange to the smallest detail all that is necessary for us to experience miracles.

Chapter 12

My Cosmic Gift Of Ancient Wisdom Cards

Names in this story have been changed to protect people's anonymity.

In 2011 my husband was given short-term employment in China and I was able to accompany him. On the day we received confirmation of the job I sent up a prayer to the Universe asking that someone I could trust turn up to house and animal sit while we were away. I didn't want to have to pack up my home and put our cats into a cattery for work that was limited to a few months.

In the evening of that same day I went to pick up my friend Holly to attend our weekly psychic development class. Holly, who is of Maori descent, didn't really need to attend, she was already quite psychic. Our class was more of a social event where we could mingle with like-minded people and learn some new things along the way.

I picked up Holly in front of the pizza place across the road from where she lived with one of her daughters and her grandchildren. No sooner had she buckled up and we had moved back into the traffic and were under way than she informed me that she needed to find a new place to live and she thought she would like to live on her own for the first time in her life. I froze. I had only just asked for someone I could trust to house sit and here she was. I told her of my husband's job and my prayer and asked if she would like to hold the fort in our absence. We struck a mutually beneficial deal and in no time at all Holly moved in and we left for China.

That year, 2011, was also the first year of a four-year formal shamanic training I had undertaken. I was studying with an American shaman and it was expected that, if possible, I would travel to the States once or twice a year. I worked online and had a mentor who I contacted weekly so it was possible to travel and still keep up my training. In June I set out from China to New Mexico meeting up with my relative Marie in Los Angeles on the way. We were both studying shamanism together and how that all came about is another story altogether.

Marie and I had the same first year mentor, Dawn. We arrived at the event in New Mexico. All our peers were there and we enjoyed a spiritually rich and mystical few days in each other's company. Dawn told us she had a pack of cards that she used daily to inspire and guide her, and she recommended them to Marie and I. Dawn felt they would resonate with us in particular as the card and book set were created by a New Zealand man, Barry Brailsford (his real name). They're called *Wisdom of the Four Winds* and are described as Shamanic Wisdom Cards, Journeys into Ancient Wisdom, beautifully illustrated by Cecilie Okada, (her real name). In short, cards from the Southern Hemisphere just like Marie and I.

Dawn very kindly offered to let us have the set for the night stressing that they were to be returned in the morning. All went well, Marie had the cards first and became engrossed by them, she began making notes. This went on for most of the evening. I had a quick look for a few minutes but I was aware that Marie was quite enchanted by the teachings in the cards and I thought I could get a longer look at them in the morning before we returned them. Like Marie I was fascinated by this fresh knowledge and did desire a deeper interlude with the set. The following morning after breakfast we had a few hold-ups to this program. First, we saw a snake in the garden and stopped to ensure that the relevant people dealt with this. Then we were enthralled by a hummingbird feeding at a feeder set up for them. No hummingbirds live in Australia and we were amazed by this delightful little creature.

Finally, we returned to our cabin and Marie hastened to finish taking notes from the book. Thus for a few reasons I never did get a good run at those cards before we returned them. I was a little peeved for a short time then decided not to worry about it as I felt that Marie really seemed to get a great deal from them. I could perhaps read her notes, and I would no doubt receive the teachings I was meant to get anyway. From that point on I was not remotely ruffled by the process that had taken place. I let it all go from my mind not even asking to look at Marie's notes.

Shortly after my return to China my husband's job finished and we flew home to Australia. I had alerted Holly of our upcoming arrival and she had found somewhere else to live and was out of our home when we got there. Holly had left something though. It was in the study, quite visible on the middle shelf of an otherwise empty cupboard. An unopened set of *Wisdom of the Four Winds* by Barry Brailsford. I was absolutely amazed. I phoned Holly to let her know of her oversight. Her reply: "I don't know how that happened but I have so many card sets I don't even know why I bought that one. Why don't you keep it." It must be noted that at no time previously had I mentioned the cards to her.

The card set I had really wanted to look at when I was in America was waiting brand new and unopened in my study in Australia when I returned home. Think about it, this was way beyond coincidental. How many different card sets would there be in the known Universe and how amazing was it that the very ones I wanted were waiting at home for me? How strange is it that of all of Holly's belongings only this beautiful card/book combination was overlooked when she departed? Even though the set was very obviously placed in the study in a cupboard that she had removed other things from when leaving.

I use it daily, the wisdom in it resonates with me. There is just one little thing: the book has been assembled incorrectly. I have to turn it upside down and back to front in order to read it. It makes me laugh, a tailor-made gift for me, a Heyoka or Sacred Clown energy. Heyoka is one who speaks, moves and reacts from an oppositional perspective to the norm. What the Tibetans call Crazy Wisdom. Heyoka is thought of as being backwards, forwards and upside down, contrary in nature, (*Wikipedia*). For me, contrary in nature often truly points the way to the wisdom of understanding the flexible potential and actualities of the reality we experience.

The power of Heyoka is to make us examine our beliefs, our fears and hatreds and to shift to new perspectives, and hence, new creative opportunities within our lives.

Why was I rewarded/gifted in such a precise and magical manner? Magical from the point of view of phenomenon not yet explicable by science. The Universe, God, the Cosmos, Divinity, Great Spirit, whatever label you attach to a power greater than self, acknowledges our smallest efforts to act with consciousness and integrity. Although I had wanted a closer examination of the *Wisdom of the Four Winds* when in America, I had moved into the correct vision of generosity and acceptance. I had not acted from the mistaken belief that to be generous to another being might cost me something. I had acted from a perspective that the Great Spirit would deliver to me the knowledge and wisdom that I was meant to receive at the time I was meant to receive it. This is precisely what occurred.

The delivery of the *Wisdom of the Four Winds* set cemented within me the understanding that the Universe is a giving entity, and as I am an aspect of the Great Spirit it is correct to comprehend that I will never be depleted in any way when I act with generosity, acceptance and kindness. In truth there is no cost to generosity.

Oh, did I mention that I also got bumped up from overbooked economy class to business class on the return flight from Los Angeles to Shanghai? This upgrade only occurred because despite being concerned that I would be unable to board the flight I once again relaxed into a correct perspective that what was in my best interest would take place. It is an abundant, loving Universe that is fully interactive with our consciousness as in truth it is the one consciousness or life, in all life. The degree to which we are able to comprehend and act from this loving perspective is what determines our experience of reality.

Chapter 13

It's a Giving World

It always comes as a surprise to me that many people who decide to join a dream circle don't in fact recall their dreams. It is as if they know they are being denied an integral part of their own consciousness.

In a dream circle a small merry group will gather at the appointed hour ready to reap the rich harvest that the dreaming hours provide. Some will already have brilliant recall and insight, however, nearly always there will be the one or two who can't remember anything. I offer the usual recommendations, keep a journal or voice recorder beside the bed. Set your intent, let your brain know you are ready to recall your dreams and grow your knowledge of life and self. Place mugwort under your pillow, create a dream bundle and place it on your altar if you have one, or beside your bed if you don't. On waking write down anything – how you feel as you greet the day, even a word or two you may recall, colours, songs, anything.

If circle members return continuously with no dreams to report then we look at the last dream they remember, even if that was in childhood. This often works, as though it reawakens your connection with the Universe and your own soul.

One notable incident that is a brilliant example of just how ready the Universe is to respond to even the slightest inclination towards exploration of dream consciousness occurred with just such a person as I have mentioned. A charming and successful healer and spiritual seeker, well versed in many aspects of holistic health and wellbeing who didn't recall her dreams.

In about the second or third dream circle she attended a wonderful thing happened. When it came to her turn to share she said she had virtually nothing, just two words recalled on waking – dog and paint. "How could these two words mean anything at all of any importance?" she asked. Everyone looked at each other for clues as I caught my breath and marvelled at what had just happened. For I knew the meaning of these two words and so I proceeded to outline what her dream words meant to me.

On the previous weekend I had been in the city, some four hours from my home town. I love a city visit, so much variety, and Melbourne is a fabulous place. Bookstores, organ recitals, restaurants, art gallery, State Library and gorgeous gardens all beckon to me. On this occasion I wandered into a store and bought a small set of very bright paints, almost electric neon hues, just what I had been looking for. I trotted out one very happy lady and walked about two stores further down the street where I came across a man begging for money – to buy paints. He was busy drawing a portrait on the pavement, which was rather good, and he was accompanied by a large dog.

Immediately I knew what was expected of me. I did put up a slight resistance as I loved those paints I had only just purchased. However, anyone who knows the voice of spirit knows that resistance isn't in your best interest and only leads to incessant nagging – nothing can nag like spirit. After a few "do I have to" and firm spirit replies of "give him the paints", I leant forward and placed my brand new paintbox on the ground in front of him. To be honest I don't think he was all that impressed, I suspect that he actually wanted cash for other things.

I walked on a little further, quietly lamenting my paints, then turned into a Myer department store where I was brought to a complete standstill by a huge sign just inside the door and to the right. It read:

It's a Giving World

Those two seemingly random words, dog and paint, in fact connected me instantly to a recent event that had been a spiritual reminder for me of how bountiful, resourceful and abundant the Universe is.

When we circle together we can dream together. The dreams spill into our reality. The joint essence of our consciousness becomes apparent and we can grasp just the smallest edge of understanding that perhaps only One of Us is truly here.

Dreams are a gift from your infinite self to the fragment in this reality that believes it is all there is. They tell us how magnificent we are, how infinite our consciousness is and that we are the miracles we seek.

Chapter 14

The Heart Of Things

Setting off on a walk, I make the decision on the outward journey to chant a recent mantra given by spirit:

> Awaken
> Holy Heart
> Perfect Being
> All is Well.

Needless to say I am chanting this, for the most part, internally. Not a good look walking along talking to yourself. If I am absolutely certain no one is around I risk chanting out loud simply because there is power in the voice. On this occasion there was a bit of both internal and external chanting. On the return trip home I stop chanting and proceed to listen to the Universe and my guides and to look around me at the wonder of this world.

I become aware of a blue light to my left accompanying me and since it is obviously conscious I ask it to tell me of its divinity, its knowing of the heart of things. Quick as a wink it replies; 'My divinity is your divinity.' Of course I think, how silly of me to seek to separate the Cosmic Consciousness, the one life in all life.

I get to the corner of my street and turn along it, a voice says to me, "Cross the road and walk on the other side." I am a Taurean and hence a tad stubborn. "I don't usually walk on that side," I reply. "I don't think it is the legal side to walk on," I add, as if that actually mattered on a very quiet rural road. I heaved a sigh and told myself to stop being a twit and I crossed the road.

There, amongst a sea of small stones was a stone simply begging to be seen – a beautiful heart shaped stone with what appeared to be a snake winding across it. Snakes are that fascinating symbol of transformation, and they tap into the realm of vibration and use it. A friend who later viewed my find thinks it is, additionally, an ouroboros, a snake eating its own tail, symbolising infinity or wholeness and creation energy, one of the oldest mystical symbols in the world.

I love that it is also the same heart shape that I tend to draw, much larger on the left or feminine side.

Mostly this beautiful stone is a statement that divinity, source, consciousness, God or whatever one wishes to call the heart of things, is always listening and aware of even the smallest of beings in an infinite universe and waiting to tell us of its omnipresence. Everything that we are or that appears to be separate from the self is actually interactive simply because it is all the one thing, the one life in all life, the one consciousness living its own perfection.

The Holy Heart is a state of being that exists within all matter, the state of Oneness. It is both the creator and the creation as it is all the one living love that is being, that exists. Consequently, all illusion falls away when the Holy Heart or void within our atomic structure is activated into 3D being. When we turn within to that one eternal heart then the world around us responds and we can and do experience the magic possibilities within the structure of our existence as Oneness.

Chapter 15

The Oddest Thing

Early one afternoon I decided to indulge in a meditation session. Settling into a large comfortable armchair in our family room I closed my eyes. My husband was in the kitchen behind me with only the benchtop between us, no wall.

As I was rather tired I presume I had nodded off as a large head floated suddenly into the room. It could best be described as a black dog's head but with very short thick hair and very small but remarkably bright and intelligent eyes. Whilst this is as close as I can come to a description it doesn't quite catch the reality. Although asleep the dream was taking place in the same time and place that was my reality, in the family room.

I became aware that my husband, still behind me in the kitchen, was scared. This was a telepathic communication. 'Don't worry,' I said, 'it is only interested in what is bad, you can let it in.' I meant he could let it into his head. As soon as I said this it was in my head. A pulsing pressure began, slowly building to a point where I thought I am not sure I can take much more of this. With this thought the pressure immediately stopped and the presence withdrew.

Still 'asleep', I hear what I know is a spaceship power up above the house then take off. All the sparrows that we feed regularly in the courtyard exploded into a noisy flurry as a result of the spaceship departure, and this woke me.

Very little time had passed and I began to tell my husband, who was still in the kitchen, what had happened. I told him of letting the 'dog' into my head and how the pressure had built up. As I opened my mouth to tell him of the spaceship I heard a voice say, 'No, don't tell him, ask him.' I understood what was wanted and so I said to my husband, "What do you think happened next?" Without a second's delay he said, "A spaceship powered up above the house then took off."

Now there really is no obvious connection between a disembodied floating dog's head with the ability to infiltrate one's mind and a spaceship above the house. One doesn't lead logically to the next.

After more than six decades on the planet at the time of writing, I am exceptionally aware of how strange this particular event is, even among the regular experiences of the non-ordinary. Long have I hesitated about putting it to paper and it is not something that I tend to tell others about. You see, for me this actually happened, I am convinced of its reality.

Although apparently asleep I had been lucid, and this experience stayed with me whilst my husband quite quickly lost clarity around this event. An odd thing that struck me was that we both called the vehicle a spaceship not a UFO which would have been the normal choice for both of us. Now I tend to lean towards the concept that whatever was traversed was interdimensional space.

I remained intrigued by this 'dream' and I knew that something had actually been done to my brain. It was several months later, when I was reading *Women Who Run With The Wolves* by Clarissa Pinkola Estes PhD, that I came across the business of sin eaters. My whole body was injected with an energetic charge as I knew suddenly beyond any doubt that I had been visited and treated by a sin eater.

I am not religious at all and don't subscribe to the standard definition of sin. Perhaps sin is really the accumulated blockages and barriers to our divine perfection that are caused by our belief in our separation from Source and hence each other. Sin could also be the subsequent actions we take based on that erroneous belief. It might potentially be said that sin is:

Separation
Induced
Nonsense

Looking back on this 'dream' I often ponder just what it removed from me, what belief needed to be removed, what blockage untangled that I might better discern my Oneness with all Life? A blessed life indeed.

Chapter 16

Look Away

As I started off on my walk I thought how much I would like to find an unusual feather, I haven't had a feather gift for some time.

About 10 minutes into the walk I come across a dead baby rabbit on the road. The body looked intact, I walked onto the road and picked up its cold stiff body by the hind legs. Blood had run from its nose and mouth but it looked like it was a quick death.

I continued to the other side of the road where I never walk normally due to the bush coming right up to the roadside making it unsafe to walk there. I placed its body in the bush bordering the road.

As I stepped across the leaf filled gutter I looked down on a feather quite unlike any I have previously been gifted. Placing the rabbit's body at the base of a tree, I said prayers to assist its energy in the next stage of being then picked up the odd feather on my way back to 'my' side of the road. I wondered if it belonged to a domestic bird. I have an arrangement with the Great Spirit that I remove dead creatures from the road if their bodies are intact. This stops those that come to eat their flesh from being injured also. The prayers are part of the honouring of all life. If I had not abided by the agreement, in all likelihood I would not have received the beautiful feather.

There are times when the magic of life flirts coquettishly with our silly belief of being divided and separated from all-encompassing consciousness. I shared this experience on social media and received a number of replies.

It was obvious that most of the comments were about the feather. Please, don't misunderstand, this is in no way a judgement of the people who commented and who were trying to help. It is, however, an observation on our difficulty in discussing anything, no matter how small, outside the bounds of 'normal'. Only two people commented on the spiritual nature of the post. Now, I had wondered what family of birds the feather was from but I hadn't asked for help with this. I did appreciate learning it was a guinea fowl feather. My friends were very helpful. Yet feather identification wasn't the point of the post. Perhaps in this fast moving digital age not many actually read the full post. However, the account of my experience was designed to illustrate the interactive nature of consciousness, to raise questions as to the nature of reality.

The creative and synchronistic nature of the experience was expected to commence a discussion on life itself. Why did I request an unusual feather on this morning? What intelligence was aware that such a feather had already been so precisely placed? Yet, was that feather in place or moved upon my request? What intelligence could find and move it, again, with such precision? If I had not stuck to my agreement to move bodies from the road I would not have been gifted the feather. Or would I have been gifted another unusual feather, or even the same feather, whatever I chose? What does this say about our lives in general? What does it say about the 'agreements' we make with whatever power we deem to be greater than ourselves? What does it say about the interactive nature of life itself? Did some aspect of the greater me know that an unusual feather had been so beautifully placed? Why does such an experience not create awe and wonder in the minds of those who hear it? Why are we so frightened of honouring the miraculous? Why do we hide from the spiritual nature of daily life? Why don't we choose to discuss non-ordinary things? The questions just multiply the more consideration one gives to the experience of intelligence existing beyond matter. Or even more amazing, that energy is actually all that is and must be conscious?

This episode reminded me of a very odd experience I had some years ago when we lived at the other end of the State. I had just exited a café and was walking towards the public toilet nearby, too many cups of tea having necessitated the visit. There was a man walking just ahead of me, apparently also on his way to the toilet block. He had the strangest energy, or to put it in a more acceptable framework, something about him fascinated me. I had no intention of taking my eyes off him yet suddenly I was aware that my eyes had slid away from him, I was looking off to the right. It annoyed me when I realised this and I literally thought, 'hang on, I wanted to watch him.' I turned my eyes back towards him only to discover he had vanished.

Now I was at a loss as to how this happened. I scanned the entire area quickly. There had not been enough time for him to have reached the male toilets on the left side of the block. He could have just made it to the disabled toilet that sat in the middle of the block and with which he had been aligned when I looked away – but not enough time for him to have entered it. Indeed, the door was open and I could see there was no one in there, I could see into the base of the cubicle and no feet were visible.

Very confused I continued on to the right and stood in line for the female toilets. I was standing just inside the door as the queue was long. I turned my head and looked out the door in time to see the same man walk into the disabled toilet. Adrenaline surged through me. When I walked out quickly the toilet door was still open and obviously empty. At the time I briefly considered walking through the open doorway of the disabled toilet but was scared to do so.

That night I dreamt of a strange group of five men with a leonine appearance, their hair more like a mane and the odd colour of a lion, not quite human but humanoid. There was no way of telling them apart, they were identical. They stood closely together in front of the toilet block and I heard a voice say that, 'the portal is now sealed and guarded'.

It has always been my understanding that this is precisely what occurred – a portal was open and in use at a toilet block of all places. It is understood that this is amazing and difficult to accept, and that the feelings and observations on the day are not available to the reader. Skeptics would have a field day with it no doubt. In my defence I can only state that as a result of a long lifetime of experiencing the far from normal, things of non-ordinary dimensions are happening more frequently to me, somewhat like a snowball gathering size and speed as it rolls down a slope. As far as I am concerned this is a life experience of mine, as real as any other.

Now, one of the things that really struck me about this event was that I had looked away from the man even though I had not wanted to. Despite my keen interest in him I found my vision wandering way off course. It was as if I had obeyed some hidden command to...look away. One can't help but wonder how often the command is given to look away from anything slightly unusual, unexpected, non-ordinary. What gives such a command? How is this diversion of intent accomplished? Does this same subconscious command also apply to us discussing the odd and unusual? Are 'look away and be quiet'...programmed into us, and if so, how and by whom? Is it part of what results in people commenting on a feather rather than the precise placing of that feather upon request? Is it an inbuilt evolutionary safety device? Does it keep us safe from ridicule, from actual physical harm or from being ostracised by our community, families and friends? Is it partially a reflection of certain religious perspectives that encompass the belief in so called demons or a devil?

If scientists are correct that we really only understand less than about 5 per cent of the Universe, does this situation of deliberate avoidance of the non-ordinary stand as a conditioned response to the other more than 90 per cent of unexplained phenomenon? Truly what concerns me is that I looked away against my will; What could possibly be behind that? Think about it, *please, think about it.*

Or perhaps I could present you with a more acceptable non-ordinary event that will tease and pull at the hems of your understandings of reality. Again, it has to be accepted that this is a true rendition of my experience of life. It is, however, a much more common experience generally than that of a portal in a public toilet, or at least I presume it is. Precognitive dreaming is a worldwide reported phenomenon. In some cultures it is taken very seriously and acted upon. One famous example is President Abraham Lincoln dreaming of seeing a coffin in the White House just a week or two prior to his assassination.

My daughter has a 10-year-old dog called Wombat. She has had him since he was a puppy. He has never run away. I have no recall of ever dreaming of him in the last decade. One Sunday night I dreamt he ran away from home and we were all searching in the wrong direction. I actually made a mental note to call my daughter and tell her to keep an eye on him but forgot about it shortly after rising early Monday morning. That evening I received a call from my very distressed girl telling me that Wombat was missing. Although it was dusk we all went out looking for him, and remembering about the direction being wrong, I went to places I might not otherwise have searched – all to no avail. Later that evening after my daughter posted a lost dog notice on Facebook she got Wombat back safe and sound. He had gone north from his home and played on a very busy highway and we searched in the south.

Seriously, give this some thought. Nothing had changed to subconsciously indicate that Wombat might decide to go see the world. No prior history indicated that he was likely to leave home, in fact rather the opposite – an anxious little boy who is a definite home lover. How is it possible that I dreamt of something quite specific that then happened the following day? In what possible way could this information have been available? What does it say of time? What does it say of free will, or of canine choice? If I hadn't had a very early Zoom conference to attend I would have written the dream down and called my daughter later in the morning. Would that have changed the outcome? What intelligence could know we would search in the wrong direction? If we paid more attention to our dreams could we avoid other unpleasant events? Could we be offered opportunities in this fashion too? Many inventions come about as the result of problem-solving dreams, and many people have won money on racehorses due to dreaming of the winner's race number, jockey's colours or horse's name. How does such a phenomenon occur? What is the as yet unknown science behind the extraordinary? Is consciousness all pervading? Is it in fact fundamental to life? Once again, the list of questions goes on and on.

If we had any true consideration of the testimony of human experience we would have to be looking at and talking about the non-ordinary happenings in life very frequently and with focus. An estimated 60 per cent of people have such experiences, that's a majority. Could discussion around such things that honoured rather than ridiculed be a step toward a more harmonious world? In fact, the list of questions that come to mind with listening to and honouring the extraordinary is huge. The value to be harvested from human experience is immense and vastly underestimated in the domain of the non-ordinary experience.

It would be true to say that I am asking that should something go bump in your world that you pay it heed, look at it, talk about it, harvest what it gifts you, be brave and jettison your beliefs in the face of extraordinary personal experience. Always remember that to be a skeptic means to have an open mind not a set of immovable beliefs.

POSTSCRIPT:

It is late 2020 as I write this, a year that for various reasons has breached even my sacred practice and anxiety has crept into my body. I have indeed become a little lost in the beliefs of this dualistic realm.

I rarely walk now on the stretch of road that was the subject at the beginning of this tale but on this day I decide to walk the old route. Nearly at the point of turning home again and very lost in the magic of wisdom poetry being gifted to me, I lift my head to see a hare lying dead in the middle of the road. There is a large pool of very bright blood surrounding his head and I say out loud that I am not moving this gory body. It occurs to me that his death is very recent and I can't help but notice that most of his body is untouched and so very beautiful. The fur is almost golden and glints where the sun kisses it.

A car is approaching and I walk to the middle of the road and pick up the hare. I continue to the other side of the road, where as we all know, I don't walk normally. As I place his body under a tree I pick up a guinea fowl feather that is waiting serenely in the grass for me. Now I have two. After performing the prayers to guide his spirit onwards in peace I am swept with awe at the precision of this miraculous event. A tear escapes and slides down my face as I express my appreciation of such a gift at a time of need for me. It encourages me further to hear something whisper, 'Walking the borders of bliss.' That is part of being shaman I think – tidying up things on the mortal side, in the realm of matter, for those who are now returned into knowing their perfection.

Chapter 17

An Interesting Week

A short summary of a week in my life early in the escalating pandemic time on Earth.

Clairaudience is my common walking ground in the spiritual realm. On the 23rd of March I heard the 60th short poem in a sequence on I AM:

I AM
the joy
of hearts undivided.

Normally I hear poetry that is spiritually instructive but on this day the tables turned and I was asked two questions.
    The first: What is the power of Now?

Presence is the simple answer, the creative presence of consciousness only works in the now, the present, that is why it is also the word for gift. Consciousness is always now, never in tomorrow – which is now when it arrives – nor in the past where it has been. Tomorrow and the past don't actually exist, time itself is just a construct then, it is always Now and the presence is always present. Hence the power of now is the presence and the infinite creativity of that conscious presence. The borderlands of time and matter fall before the presence.

Then, as happens with so many spiritual questions, the other option rears its head. What is the power of what is happening now in this pandemic climate of fear and anxiety?

For me it grants the time for reflection, the space to create a new vision of myself, to re-evaluate the me, and hence the world, I want to be. It reminds me that every single choice I make fashions my experience of this world. Thus, I am in the enviable position of being free to choose differently. I can investigate what beliefs and ideas I have that are detrimental to peace, harmony, compassion and kindness. What do I truly wish to be? What is the most important thing in my expression of my own self? The power of now, for me, is the power to embrace brave new visions of myself and to take the necessary steps to allow this new, balanced and glowing me to be birthed.

The second question: What is the name of heaven?

"Well seriously, I thought heaven was the name of heaven," I responded. I gave it some more thought and could only come up with: home. Our true home I thought. I pondered, not for the first time and certainly not likely to be the last, my sanity. Yet I was left feeling incomplete and found this a perplexing question to be asked. Until the following morning.

In my email inbox was my regular Word of the Day from the Merriam Webster Dictionary. The word was welkin – what on earth is that? I thought.

Welkin means: 1a) vault of the sky, firmament. 1b) the celestial abode of God or the gods: heaven.

It even mentioned that a carol we sing as 'Hark the herald angels sing' was originally worded, 'Hark, how all the welkin ring.'

The name for heaven appeared in my email box, welkin. If taken simply it could mean well kin or family, that place or state where we know and live our oneness, where we comprehend fully what 'the one life in all life' means. For surely we are well when we understand being an individuated aspect of one life and that every aspect of that individuation, be it animal, plant, mineral, energy or inter-dimensional, is our family? Does this make heaven/welkin a state of being that we can choose to enact?

Of course, the glaring question is what intelligence asked the question of me and then provided the answer for me in such a tech savvy mode of operation? Surely the provision of the answer could be seen as an example of that state of Oneness simply being? The orchestration is amazing.

The 25th of March brought a cautionary tale for those of us who pay attention to dreams and a heads up about their relevance to those who don't.

As I was treating myself to a little nanna nap I both heard and saw a four-word sentence, it wasn't in English. As I had only just closed my eyes I still felt 'awake' and repeated the sentence to myself a few times and was sure I would remember it. Sometime later I surfaced and realised I had forgotten the third word. After a few moments of concentration it came back, Heide. Did I then write the sentence down? No, I went back to sleep, silly me. When I woke up later I had lost the first and last words. I still recalled the second word as it had been the only one I recognised, Odin, the Norse God. I researched Heide and discovered that this is one of the names of a Norse goddess. The language was Norse and I am left kicking myself for losing the connecting or message related words of the sentence. Yet it brought to mind the previous days Welkin, abode of the Gods. Now I am hearing Norse names of gods and goddesses. *Lesson: write down dreams immediately.*

Also, on this date I received a short poem that went into my file of Spirit Sentences, again about 60 or so

The Joy of all
that is
belongs to
the Heart that gives.

Nearly forgot this little gem from the 26th of March, 2020:

On a journey to the chemist for a much needed item my husband requested I go to the supermarket opposite the chemist and buy him a bag of potato chips, crisps for my US friends. The request had been refused but having made my purchase at the chemist I relented and decided to buy the chips. As I walked out the chemist door I 'saw' the toilet paper aisle in the supermarket and it had a few packets of toilet paper on a shelf. This was about 4pm and there has been nothing but empty shelves in that aisle for weeks now past the usual early morning stampede. We had been all right for toilet paper as I had purchased some just before it had become an endangered species. However, I had been thinking that I needed to keep an eye open for some soon. So when I 'saw' the aisle with packets on a shelf I listened to that voice that told me to pop a gold light around the packets and that would keep one for me.

Still thinking this was a virtual impossibility, I approached the supermarket door and a lady came out with a trolley containing a 10-pack of that fabulous stuff...toilet paper. A fluke I thought, an employee who had kept one from the morning delivery for herself. I entered the store and obeying my instincts turned to the left and made towards the aisle in question. I passed numerous people with 10-packs in their trolleys or under their arms. My speed increased and whilst I kept my dignity and did not break into a run I was probably speed walking for Australia when I turned into the aisle I needed and saw at the other end the exact arrangement of toilet paper on one shelf that I had 'seen' just a minute or so previously. Sure enough I happily collected my allotted 10-roll pack, tucked it safely under one arm and made my way to the chip aisle for Rod's little treat which was well deserved I decided.

It seems I had indeed kept an eye open for toilet paper, my third eye.

On today's walk, March 28, 2020, my long gone Mum's birthday, I asked one of my contacts for the one thing I most need to know in order to manifest my own divinity. Within moments I pass a house with music blaring, it is Queen and the line I hear is, "open your eyes, look up to the skies and see".

Theme for the week, Queens/Goddesses, Kings/Gods and heaven.

Queens, powerful feminine characteristics emerging into consciousness.

Kings, wealth of knowledge, recognition of inner power, awareness of self-worth.

God/Goddess Love, light, truth, creative power, oneness, wisdom, infinity, master teacher within all.

Looking up to the skies could mean the firmament, the vault of heaven, the welkin, that state of perfection that always is and from which we are drawn and to which we return. See the inherent truth in being, take my eyes away from illusion.

Add to this a small dream of birthing a dragon and guarding myself and the baby dragon, literally being both the birther and the guardian. I sense a balancing of power and the rising of kundalini energy into a new state of being that is more harmonious and a truer reflection of humanity's divine essence. Given the carer role it seems that this new rising energy will require us to nurture and protect it for some time so that it is able to grow.

When mature, it will spread its message of peace and compassion, dropping little treasures of wisdom into the pools of our hearts, the ripples flowing out and through all hearts.

All in all, a good week full of spiritual blessings and love.

Chapter 18

Oneness, Dreams and Waterlilies

My alarm was set for 5.50am as I facilitate a Zoom dream group every second week. I woke at 5.15am and decided to go back to sleep until the alarm sounded. In the magical mystical land of the hypnopompic state I was gifted a remarkable short dream.

I was viewing a very large oval shaped pond filled with the leaves of water lilies and lotus. The water at the edge was crystal clear and moving slightly, and I heard that the water was conscious and completely self-reliant, made of itself by itself. The most amazing sentence was spoken to me; "The whole world wants you to live." I woke to the alarm.

The dream being so clear and odd I researched the symbols, particularly of the lotus and the water lily.

They share some symbolic attributes: both denote purity and rebirth amongst a myriad of other things. For instance, I learnt that according to legend, Gautama Buddha's first steps made lotus flowers appear everywhere he stepped. The word oval, the shape of the pond in the dream, is derived from the Latin *ovum* from which we get egg, a shape that represents rebirth, fertility and even immortality. Also, a zest for life. Ponds are pure reflective and tranquil spaces. Water is emotion, life and transcendence of the earthly condition.

During my Zoom dream circle I reminded participants to look for synchronicities in their waking lives that resonate with their dreams.

Most of my morning was spent spontaneously singing, "I've got the whole world in my hands." It was hours before I recalled that it is a hymn about Christ and goes; "He's got the whole world in his hands."

Due to a wonderful catch up with a friend I didn't undertake my usual walk until after lunch. This is my form of moving meditation and before long I heard the following short poem:

> In Loving Oneness
> illusion's lies are not told
> and thus all error
> is resolved.

-
About a kilometre out from home I stopped to talk to three white cockatoos. Then, as I took a few steps more,

I came across a box filled with waterlilies and a sign propped against it advised they were free and to, 'please help yourself.' I had just looked at my phone and the time was 1.11pm. I still had quite some way to walk and continued on for a few more steps. Then it hit me, waterlilies, free. How many times in all my years of walking in places and countries various had I come across a box of free waterlilies, let alone on the day I had received a remarkable dream about them? Never. I returned to take a photo of the lilies and the sign.

Then I walked on. However, it occurred to me that this was an incredible gift and so I decided that if there were any lilies remaining on my return I would take one home, despite the fact that they were sitting in water and even the smallest pot looked heavy. Also, I had nothing to carry one in. A silent prayer to save one for me was sent to the Universe.

I walked fast and on my way home I discovered that they were all still sitting there. I picked the one that felt right to me and trotted off home with a dripping pot plant that was indeed heavy and difficult to carry. By then I couldn't wipe the grin off my face. What a blessed life I lead, it was only a few days prior to this that I woke with the sentence, "I am wired for being blessed" in my mind.

The truth is we are ALL wired for being blessed, however our belief in being separate from each other and all other forms of life blocks us from experiencing the miraculous. The veils between the realms are thin and dissolve like mist in the sun when we begin to comprehend that it is the one life in all life with infinite creative diversity available to it. Make room in the heart for the miracles of that one loving consciousness.

My husband was having a little nap, I had told him about the dream as it was so beautiful. Now I could hardly wait to see the expression on his face when he gets up to find a water lily sitting in the kitchen sink.

PART TWO

I had thought that all things water lily were done with, however three nights after the original dream I had another.

In the second dream I am attending a shamanic event being held by the woman whose Mystery School I had attended for honing my shamanic skills. After listening to her talk I withdraw to another room where other event participants are taking a break. Someone says that our teacher is not as on the ball as usual and I reply that I think if anything she is sharper than in years previous. A man agrees with me. An old friend, Feather, and I hug. She is about to leave and I send my love to her partner Raven and their cat Lily. I check with Feather that this is the cat's name. (This is true in waking life, their cat is called Lily.) Feather comes back into the room, she is flustered. A man has given her a box to give to whoever suggested that the cat should be called Galea after a Lily. I say it was me. Everyone is a bit concerned/scared

– this man is a very powerful shaman – we can all feel his power but he never enters the room. Feather says I have to sign for the box. I can't find a docket but then see it is stuck to the underside of the box. I decide to sign in an old way that I used years ago but the paper folds over and the signature is quite illegible which I am pleased about. I feel it would be unwise to give this man all the truth of me.

Research of Galea provides the information that it is a structure shaped like a helmet. Among other things it is also a tough fibrous sheet of connective tissue that extends over the cranium, the middle or third layer of the scalp.

Although some lilies are poisonous, my research had also uncovered the information that certain lilies and lotuses have psychoactive properties. Somehow, I find myself on a page devoted to Mayan use of the white water lily, Nymphaea Ampla. Mayan paintings denote it springing from the back of crocodiles swimming in water. (I have strong non-ordinary associations with reptiles and have since childhood.) However, staggeringly the association between the black jaguar and this water lily is especially dominant. My shamanic power animal is a black jaguar...a big cat. There are paintings of jaguars wearing the stalks and buds of the lily as a head ornament, or dancing with water lilies. The water lily also appears on vessels that depict visionary scenes from the underworld. The water lily appears to invoke shamanic ecstasy and the shaman undergoes transformation.

There is even a Mayan hieroglyph known by the name jaguar-water lily. Some consider the jaguar-water lily to mean a transformed shaman. In the region concerned, the jaguar is considered the most important shamanic animal and/or is the animal that is identical to the shaman and whose shape he can assume.

There is a Mayan glyph called the *uay* glyph which shows a jaguar swimming in a lake. The word *uay* literally means transformation/magic and refers to either the nagual, an animal-shaped alter ego, or a shaman who is able to shape shift.

Many years ago I attended a spiritual healer and medium, Doug Osborne, who not only made me the happy recipient of an instantaneous healing of a damaged knee but also informed me I had a South American Indian as a guide who didn't speak English. I had actually seen the guide myself in a warning vision prior to damaging that knee. I consider that this guide may have gifted me a power dream. We all tend to be wary of great non-ordinary abilities and those who can direct and control them.

Upon reflection I suspect that the remarks about my teacher – that she isn't as on the ball and that she is more powerful than ever – are indicative of my personal concerns. It has occurred to me that perhaps I am not as powerful as I once was but also that the shaman world generally isn't up to dealing with the chaos billowing out into the world globally. My higher self has answered my concerns regarding both personal and global shamanic abilities, reassuring me that in fact all is even more polished and precise than previously.

I have a strong appreciation of spiritual amphibology, statements that are ambiguous, having more than one possible interpretation – I suspect an ancient method of passing on hidden wisdoms. A part of that original sign advertising free water lilies said, 'Please help yourself'. Helping myself could mean both taking a free water lily and literally helping myself to a new level of wellbeing, be that spiritual, mental, emotional, physical or a combination of such.

Chapter 19

A Confluence of Kindnesses

Following an emotionally tumultuous few weeks in South Korea with my eldest daughter as she met her birth mother for the first time, I was happy to be back on familiar ground.

My daughter and I parted ways in Melbourne. I was staying the night and doing a bit of window and actual shopping before taking the midday train home the following day.

Several times over the previous weeks I had said to my girl that we simply needed to be kind. Thirty years is a long time to not know if one of your children is alive, happy and loved, let alone longing on a daily basis to hold your only daughter in your arms. If things had become a little intense at times it was understandable. All was made much more difficult by not sharing a language, still being denied access to the rest of her birth family and needing an interpreter.

Now I had a precious 24 hours all to myself. Time to reflect and to process all that had occurred and time to celebrate that all had gone markedly better than I had anticipated. Time to wander my beloved Melbourne with a light and happy heart even though I was aware that I didn't feel quite as physically safe here at home as I had in Seoul. There was a slightly forbidding forest or jungle energy present that was a recent addition to the urban atmosphere. Despite this I felt incredibly elevated, peaceful and in harmony with the world. In fact I am sure I was glowing to those who had the sight or necessity to perceive such a reality. Having checked in to my hotel and deposited my luggage, I ventured out again to hunt down a good feed before I hit the sack for a well-deserved night's rest.

Half a block from the hotel, as I turned a corner, I saw coming towards me a very small man, well under five feet in height. He looked a little down and the energy around him was heavy and dull. As I was about to pass him I think he saw my radiance and he hailed me. The first thing out of his mouth was a request for money. I felt myself sigh and droop slightly in response. He followed this request with a sketchy story of having just left a meeting with his wife only to discover his wallet had been stolen. Money was required in order for him to get home he told me. Flattened by the request and being perceived as a mark, I replied that I didn't have money to spare.

He slumped and some spark died in his eyes. As he so visibly deflated at my refusal I began to question if he was in fact in genuine need. I pointed out that we were opposite a huge central railway hub and suggested that he go there and explain his predicament and perhaps they could help. He could also report the theft of his wallet to the police stationed there. Immediately his mood lifted again and he said, "Do they do that?" I replied that it was worth going over to find out – nothing ventured nothing gained. Off he went leaving me to question my own responses to the situation – had I misjudged him, did I do enough if that was so? As I mulled this over I continued on my way to an aromatic and tasty vegetarian Indian meal prior to returning to the hotel.

I was up bright and early the next day and after checking my luggage into the railway station, I was left with an entire morning to roam my favourite inner-city haunts. I crossed to the tram stop in the middle of the road just a few steps from the place of my encounter on the previous evening. A tram had just departed and walking towards me was the sole remaining occupant on the platform, an elderly woman using a walking frame. Her still striking face was surrounded by a cascade of wavy grey hair that looked as though it may never have been fully tamed. She stopped me and in a voice liltingly tinged with the accents of Poland informed me that she was a little lost. After she finished explaining where she was going I realised that she was indeed not in the correct place to catch the appropriate tram to the destination she required.

I thought she might need the next intersecting stop down from us and I offered to walk with her to that stop. Piercing light blue eyes searched my face as she explained that she had just been asking God for help. "Here I am, ready to help," I replied. A delighted smile erupted like sun through the mist as she said, "He has sent me a beautiful lady." At 61 I decided to accept the terms of reference as it was homage not likely to occur often from here on in. My concerns about my choices from the previous night's encounter had served to dissipate any minor concerns regarding the erosion of my planned activities. I reassured her that I had all the time in the world.

We journeyed peacefully together towards the next stop and she began to regale me with snippets from her life. Immigrants following the war, she and her husband had settled in a regional centre, worked hard and raised children with boring and appropriate Australian names. They had generally had a good life until the husband's slow decline and eventual death from dementia. She had nursed him and it had not always been easy. He had called her his Alexandria the Great she proudly informed me and by now I was beginning to concur. The next stop was not the correct one and we made our way back to our original starting point.

I understood that this was a yearly pilgrimage for her to a synagogue for a special service of some sort. A Roman Catholic herself she performed this duty as a personal tribute, an honouring and an act of solidarity. Normally a grandson accompanied her but he was nearly grown and had other plans for this weekend. With the same adventurous flame undimmed that saw her travel half a world from her home to settle and begin again, she had set out alone for a long day's travel. She had with her a Jewish prayer shawl, which she had found in an opportunity shop and that she kept for this annual event. We caught a tram to the correct connecting spot and I escorted her to await her next tram. She had a bus ride to take after that. I heard of how she still lived in the same house, still kept ducks and chooks and grew food in her garden. Alexandria had brought her lunch with her and she offered to share it with me while we waited.

The next tram arrived and I explained to the driver what bus Alexandria needed to catch after this tram and he assured me he would take care of her. After climbing the few steps she had only to sit as people had moved unasked, others had risen to take her walker and to offer support. I bid a very fond farewell to a totally charming lady and continued on my way with much less time available to me to achieve my own aims yet strangely unconcerned and remarkably light of heart. I was struck by how willing people had been to assist Alexandria, and I contemplated the idea that knowing that so many people love to show their kind hearts, she walks through life giving others the opportunity to shine a little.

Only a short walk to the city centre and then two blocks to the Theosophical Society Bookshop and all was going well. Then I saw him. Lying on the pavement, totally out to it was a relatively young homeless person with the added dank atmosphere of addiction wafting around him. He was totally dishevelled and not remotely clean of dress or person since washing facilities are few and far between for street people. I didn't even have to think about it, I knew by now that Spirit was busy with me today. I decided to get him some food for when he regained consciousness. Then, noticing how uncomfortable it seemed to have no place to rest his head other than the ground, I decided to try to buy a blow-up pillow. A normal pillow would be cumbersome to lug around and difficult to keep dry. Off I trotted to spend quite some time in an entirely fruitless blow-up pillow hunt.

Now time was truly getting short so I bought a large and very tasty looking muffin to leave near him. When I got back to him he was still out to it and I could have kicked myself for failing to buy a drink. When I realised he hadn't moved one iota since I had last seem him I began to think he might be dead. So, talking to him all the time, I put the muffin in its bag near to him and gently touched his hand, the warmth of which was truly reassuring. I smiled and said it was good he was still with us and looked up to see a young dark-haired woman watching me with a look of puzzlement mixed with surprise on her face. I smiled and she beamed back. It was good.

Once I was on the long train ride home and had time to think it seemed apparent to me that I had just completed a test around my levels of kindness and empathy. Furthermore, I was the one doing the assessment. I could have done better with the first man, although his immediate request for money may well have been an attempt to take advantage of me. If this was the case, then by setting a boundary I had in fact done the most loving thing, a refusal to be manipulated. In case his need was genuine then I had directed him to other sources of possible assistance, so altogether not too bad. The Alexandria test had been passed with flying colours. I made a mental note of the ways and means of improving the third encounter, the largest detriment to my kindness in this instance had been my lack of faith regarding the amount of time left available to me before my train departed. Kindness then must rely upon trust that the Universe itself supports the act. Another aspect I noticed was that I had no expectations of any interaction, the act of kindness was its own reward.

It was not until several months later when I started to write this that something else became blindingly obvious: it had been an archetypal heroine's journey complete with the grieving parent, lost child, elements of a strange land with a language that I couldn't speak followed by a slightly forbidding urban landscape bringing to mind forest or jungle, the little folk, the crone and last but not least the social outcast. Bulk standard normal myth just chock-a-block with the lot. After all, we are the 'one with the lot' society. The journey through the myth is where the immortal infinite conscious self surfaces into the everyday consciousness. How adept consciousness is in sensing reality and, most importantly, in seeing the oneness in all people we encounter. All such journeys not only test the initiate but those who hear the tale. What would anyone else have done in these circumstances? How developed is the ability to see all as kin, the link to kindness being to see 'others' as the self. The very judgement I pass on each case and on myself would, in truth, be unnecessary if I was at 'one'.

How do I venture further into my divine self, the cosmic me that knows what is true of any situation? How do I evolve completely into loving kindness walking through a three dimensional maelstrom of illusionary beliefs that keep the focus on separation and fear? How do I expand my conscious awareness into the truth of its perfection as immortal love? Is it really as simple as ceasing to be concerned with judgement and merely being as kind as possible in all encounters? Did my late father-in-law's affinity for an old saying in fact sum it up rather well? "Life is mostly froth and bubbles but two things stand like stone, kindness in another's troubles and courage in your own." Perhaps all that is required is that I simply keep my focus on expressing kindness and trust that I am well suited to the task and that my focus shall in all ways be supported by the very oneness that we are.

For me one thing became apparent. Beyond it all, beneath it all, what I had really been looking at was what beliefs I have that might hinder my expression of kindness in any given situation. This in itself limits the manifestation of my own divinity in the here and now. My beliefs form my perceptions then my choices, then my actions, this then forms my experience of reality. Where do these beliefs keep me from expressing a fuller version of my being? What beliefs stop me from forming a loving, peaceful, kind and compassionate world?

Chapter 20

Charm

A tiny tale indeed, hardly qualifying for a chapter but most worthy in its own right as a transformational gift. Truth is, after all, simple. What use would it be if it were not?

For many years it has been my daily practice to draw a card from either of two inspirational card sets I own. This gives me a focus for my spiritual expansion or pondering throughout the day. One day as I sat at my desk and my thought turned to what card I would draw today, I heard the word charm. Now this is not one of the cards in either deck. A quick search gives me the origins of the word; aside from the expected delighting, attracting or fascinating, other definitions were song, verse, incantation or magic spell, an act or saying believed to have power. Spell and spelling both have their origins in the old French word *espeller*, as though we have always known the power of words.

Later in the morning I took my ritual meditation walk, where the steady rhythm becomes like a bodily chant occupying my busy brain. This allows the conscious reception of the deep truth, that underlies the distracted waves of everyday life, to flow through and into my keeping. Whilst in this state I ask for my charm. Immediately I hear:

Patient Peacefulness Promulgates Perfection.

After years of spirit guidance from several intelligences I am well aware that they tend to use old fashioned terms. Always I must check the etymology of words for the meaning that corresponds to the occasion.

Patient: to suffer or bear
Peacefulness: silence, tranquility
Promulgates: proclaims: as in brings forth, makes known
Perfection: completion

My charm translates to:

Bearing silence and tranquility brings forth and makes known completion.

There is great beauty and faith or knowing in these words, in either of the forms. Repetition results in relief and relaxation at a deep level – it works like…a charm.

Chapter 21

The Gate Keeper

The inner exercise fairy wakes me with her usual precision at 6.25am. I tell her to take a hike without me. Vamoose, I've walked three times already this week, I had a late night, I'm getting old. "Leave me alone," I snarl. None of this rids me of her insistent call. I attempt to lose gracefully by making a deal. I'll go if my spirit guides will talk to me on the walk. They have been quieter in the last few days and I miss the wisdom they gift me.

Up I get, drag on dirty clothes, a sunhat, wash the remnants of sleep from bleary eyes and emerge, still half asleep, out the front door of my lovely home. The same home that houses a most comfortable bed the separation from which I continue to lament. I have my trusty camera thrust deep into a pocket to catch early light-enshrined beauty that occurs frequently on my walks to the lake.

I trudge along, say my prayers for the day, greet local magpies and the alpaca and sheep in the corner paddock, all with little enthusiasm today.

Still wafting across the wonderland between sleep and awake I hear myself internally singing a song. "How deep is my love" is playing on my inner radio. Often, as in this case, my guides will change the words of a song slightly in order to focus my attention where they desire it. Then, beneath the song, a sentence drifts past my consciousness. To my surprise I catch it and haul it back into plain view on my inner screen for examination. "I am at one with the Gate Keeper." That's the sentence.

Now I know science proved quite some years ago that women can hear and interact with two separate conversations at the one time. A function provided for motherhood I presume. Men are not so blessed. Hence they never get it that a woman can answer someone's "Where are my socks?" or similar question while still listening to the man in their life and being fully part of that conversation. Puts them at quite a disadvantage in my opinion. However, it had never previously occurred to me that the same could hold true for inner conversations. Heavens I thought, how much have I missed over the years from my own inner realms?

I turned my attention to the sentence I had randomly fished from the seas of unexplored knowing. I am at one with the Gate Keeper. Hmmm, what gate I questioned? "The gate between the worlds," I heard back. What does the Gate Keeper require of me to grant me safe passage

I wondered? Affection was the answer. I visualised myself placing a red rose into the Gate Keeper's hand. What form does the Gate Keeper take I asked? Can I have the Gate Keeper resemble whatever I like, the Guardian in the Thor movies for instance? Or maybe a bull ant such as I had passed on the path a few minutes previously – they are feisty little creatures and would make good guardians I presume. I hear the reply, "Yes, the form is fluid." Suddenly, I am not so pleased with this, it doesn't convey the truth in a fashion that assists me to make sense of this Gate Keeper.

Who is the Gate Keeper, I ask? Then the conversation becomes focused. "The Gate Keeper is an aspect of you that keeps you safe. It evaluates your ability to step past fear and to leave your beliefs and disbeliefs at the gate. How well accomplished you are at doing this determines your travel destination options and the information or wisdom that will be placed in your care."

I decide to look up the definition of the phrase 'at one' on my return home. It means a single unit, an entire thing, an entity or individual. On the same online dictionary page I find the word for the day is umbra, meaning shade or shadow, the invariable or characteristic accompaniment or companion of a person or thing. So is the Gate Keeper my umbra, or am I its? One of us the shadow of the other. Or is the Gate Keeper simply the part of the whole that stands in the shade determining the degree of enlightenment available to the entire entity?

Am I at one with my own shadow and thus free to travel dimensions and worlds beyond everyday comprehension? Is the affection I hold for my shadow an acknowledgement of its role in my journey to remembering my own Divinity?

Isn't it a fabulous thing to know that between us and other realities stands an aspect of our divine consciousness that knows precisely what experiences we are prepared to undertake safely?

Chapter 22

The Universal Science Group

I first came across one of Murdo MacDonald-Bayne's books in my late father's library. It was called *The Higher Power You Can Use*. My husband and I both enjoyed it but I didn't go hunting for any other of his works. However, when I was in my mid-30s I visited a very out of the way second-hand book shop and there, in the travel section where it certainly did not belong, a book leapt out at me. It was as if it was lit up with a light and I pounced on it – another Murdo book, called *Beyond the Himalayas.* This book outlined exactly how I had always suspected that life really worked, and I devoured it. He was an amazing spiritual teacher credited with channelling Christ for a number of talks that formed the basis of another work called *Divine Healing of Mind and Body*.

Since reading *Beyond the Himalayas* I have been a keen student of his, and find his lectures spiritually transformative. He formed the College of Universal Science.

Perusing the online College of Universal Science site, now unfortunately defunct, in order to discern what I needed to read for Level 4, I came across an old photo of Murdo MacDonald-Bayne, talking to students of his in Melbourne, circa 1940. Although I had seen this photo many times before I felt I should look again at this group. I decided to do a quick online search to see if I had missed anything in previous searches for this group and what had happened to them.

I lucked out as I came across a link to the *La Trobe Journal* from 2010. I had looked previously at an article linked to *La Trobe* but felt pressure to peruse it all again. The article was titled 'Rebuilding the Future: The Universal Science Group in Post-War Melbourne'. It transpired that all the surviving written records of the group had been donated to the State Library of Victoria. This was not the article I had seen previously and now I had fresh information.

Sometime in the 1940s Murdo had visited Melbourne to meet supporters, amongst whom were Joy and Hugh Hall, Joy's son from a previous marriage, Rex Roadknight, and Max Watkin.

Now, upon reading this I immediately decided to visit the State Library as soon as possible, the mention of other photos in the collection was quite an enticement. However, for some reason my interest focused on Rex

Roadknight and really intensified when I came across the fact that for much of his relatively short life he resided at Williams Road, Olinda in Victoria. Many years ago we had looked at a house for sale in that road and I had fallen deeply in love with the property which we were not able to purchase. I have thought of it often over the years.

My husband said he thought Roadknight would not have been a real surname but I did an ancestry check and discovered it was indeed Rex's real surname. At some point in all this I began to 'feel' Rex, as though he was aware of me searching all this out and of my interest in him.

Murdo MacDonald-Bayne has been one of the great, if not greatest, teachers of my spiritual life. Friends and I have a Murdo study group. Murdo has visited me regularly in dreams and on a psychic level and gifted me many wisdom teachings.

As I became aware of Rex as a presence during all of this, I set him a little challenge to 'prove' his actually being around me. I told him that if he managed to produce the name Roadknight from another source by the end of the following day, either I was to hear it or see it written somewhere, then I would take that as proof of his interest and presence.

In the evening of the next day my friends and I met for our regular circle, and as we usually did we had a quick catch up on everyone's week. I mentioned discovering that the State Library had a lot of data about the

Melbourne Group. Then, with some urging from spirit I told them about my husband saying Roadknight couldn't be a 'real' surname. It was barely out my mouth when my friend Jo said of course it was, it's the surname of the woman for whom she was presently house sitting! Also, the name of a well-known singer, Margaret Roadknight, the sister of the same woman. Another friend piped up with the fact that there is a street named Roadknight in an adjacent town.

So here I am at a group where three of the participants are all very interested in the works of Murdo MacDonald-Bayne – the reason we were meeting in the first place – who had a devoted Melbourne follower, Rex Roadknight, the same surname as the woman my friend Jo was house sitting for. I didn't tell them I had set a challenge as I was a bit gobsmacked really.

Seems Rex had met my challenge quite adequately and this whet my appetite for what might be awaiting me in those records at the library. Of course, it is also a wonderful encouragement in terms of the work we are attempting to do in this group and what may yet transpire from our dedication. A charming way of letting me know that Murdo and his loyal supporters are around us and assisting with our endeavours. For some reason I find it reassuring that Rex is keeping an eye on things from his side of the veil. A friend in the light.

Chapter 23

The Quantum Altar of Availability

This occurred at a time when my sleep was disrupted. Our beautiful wolfhound mastiff cross, Walter, had just had a leg amputated due to bone cancer. Despite pain medication he was having difficulties during the night and I had wakened to comfort him and settle him back down.

Rather than lie awake worrying about things I use shamanic techniques to re-enter the sleep world. On this occasion I decided to revisit an area that I had been to in a vision exercise some time ago. It is a place where one of my main spirit guides chose to meet me previously. This guide sent Walter to me, a wolf power animal made manifest. As I mentioned earlier, I had dreamt of Walter before we had acquired him or even knew of his existence.

All was going well. I had climbed a stony path to the top of the mountain in the vision. As I came over the crest and onto the plateau on the mountain top I saw before me a large stone altar. There were men standing beside it.

They informed me that I was here to sacrifice my divine heart to the Universe. Next thing I knew I am lying on the altar and thinking they are going to cut my heart out, this is going to hurt! "Oh no," says the man to my left, "there is no cutting to be done, there can be no cutting of ties between you and your divine heart." It became blindingly obvious that mankind had, in the past, perverted this ceremony by making it an act of religious power that had required the actual sacrifice of a physical being and the harvesting of their heart. This act of injustice could never be truth of Being. Truth is that I *am* my Divine Heart, I just didn't know it yet.

Immediately it was apparent that this was a sacred ceremony where I release my divine heart energy from the fetters of my small personal self thus setting it free to expand throughout all consciousness. It was no longer to be bound by my beliefs and was free to become the one heart in all hearts.

I comprehended that this sacrifice on my part, an act of courage and heartfelt faith, would return to me a wisdom of heart energy that was radically increased in magnitude and magnificence. One could even say it would be complete.

The gifting of my heart would by some magical means make me aware of my wholeness from the very smallest aspect to the infinite and immortal conscious me. We must travel within to the atomic space to find the divine heart, hence a quantum altar. Divinity lies within us. All the dross of short mortal life would be replaced by the truth of inherent perfection of being. It is a virtual impossibility to make a comparison between pre and post heart sacrifice perception. That instant agreement to surrender my heart, to make it available to the Universe, made the heart of the Universe available in return. I surrendered to Love.

Chapter 24

Dad, Books and Dreams

Gently running a finger around my upturned palm the psychic stared intently into a portal I couldn't perceive. Her eyes lifted to mine and she drew a breath, "Oh my dear, your sister, has she always been so...nasty?" A silent sob rose from my heart and broke into nothingness at the unspeakable relief that this could be seen by someone who knew absolutely nothing of my family. This fact of my experience of sisterhood stood in all its truth in some aspect of a greater reality.

The answer to that question is, as so many answers are, quite complicated. All shaded by the actions and words of parents lost in the mists of childhood, blended into so many 'if onlys' and 'might have beens'. A mishmash of dreams and hopes and memories.

Put bluntly, yes, she was often unpleasant and she directed nearly all of it at me. No one else saw it, except my mother, and it was rarely delivered to others. My arrival on the scene after she held total sway for nearly eight years came as quite a shock to her and her swiftly developing refusal to love me and consequent open hostility had my mother lying awake at night worrying over how to fix it. Mostly my sister simply pretended I wasn't there, refused to interact with me anymore than sheer necessity required or parents demanded.

When I was about 14 she married and I think decided that she should try to be more like a sister ought to be. To her credit she tried for many years, we even shared a house for six months at one point. Yet when I was 31 she informed me that she had tried to change how she felt about me and simply couldn't. I was told it was largely our father's fault for insisting that she had to love her sister and making her kiss me when I was a baby. It was only when a cousin said, decades later, that at least my sister saying this to me indicated she realised the fault was actually with her, that I was released from the dreadful self-blame and thinking that I was unworthy of her love.

From the time I was 31 things had got steadily worse, and our joint administration of our parents' affairs when I was in my late 40s was a nightmare. By the time this situation occurred my mother had advanced dementia. My father died not that long after we were forced to take over his affairs. He had suffered a psychotic break and he was placed in a nursing home. An extremely manipulative and controlling person, he simply decided to die in my opinion, as he couldn't function within the new parameters that surrounded him. Nobody had thought that my mother would survive him, let alone by a couple of years.

The same psychic who had seen the truth of my experience of sisterhood also told me, prior to the trials of clearing the family home to ready it for sale, that there existed a red book, and in that book lay some sort of proof of my sister's character. The psychic didn't know what was in the book that gave proof but insisted that it was definitive proof of her nature as far as it related to me.

My father's library was such that it took a fair amount of work to clear. My sister and I knew that a few books of his were probably of some value. We placed them together but still among the other books. My sister was only an hour's travel from the property but it took me at least four hours to get there from our regional home.

One day she phoned me to say she had been to the family home and discovered that all the valuable books were missing. She asked me if I had them and I told her I certainly did not. She then declared that they must have been stolen. I hung up. Shaking with anger I went and told my husband. By this stage of the administration we were under no delusions as to what we were dealing with but how were we to prove that she had the books herself? My husband asked me what people normally do when their belongings are stolen. I replied that they report it to the police. He said to do just that. I called my sister back, told her when I would be down and said if the books couldn't be found when I got down then I would be reporting them as stolen to the police.

Of course, the books weren't anywhere to be found. Now, if they were just any books I might not have gone to the police but the fact was that one of those books was a book on Lenin and the Russian Revolution. It was in excellent condition. It not only had a red leather cover but inside it was an armband of the revolution securely attached. It was because of this red book and the easily identifiable object within it that I proceeded to the police station.

The officer at the desk listened to my account of events. He then said that most thieves wouldn't know a valuable book from any other and it was all rather odd. He suggested that before I proceeded to filing an actual theft case that I call my sister one more time and see what happened. I called her from the police station front desk with him listening to my end of the conversation. For many minutes she insisted they were stolen before she finally got around to saying that she thought I had them. This was to make me back off as it implied I could be the one in trouble if I continued. For once in my life where my sister was concerned I stood my ground and insisted that I would be reporting the theft and getting it investigated. I added that if I had stolen them I wouldn't be standing in a police station reporting their theft. Then

I heard her husband in the background say something to her. She came back to me after a minute and said he had just told her the books concerned were in their garage. They had put them there to take them to a person locally to be valued and she must have forgotten about it! When I hung up and looked at the policeman he said to me, "Now you know your sister is a liar." All thanks to a red book with something red inside it too. Needless to say I never saw those books again. When she died they were not sent back to me. One of them I had a strong attachment to, an old dictionary. I often wonder where it ended up.

As far as the remaining books were concerned my sister had informed me she wasn't interested in them and to get rid of them however I liked. As I lifted them from the shelves I put aside quite a few that sounded interesting and I have kept them ever since but haven't really delved into them. A great reader, I always have a pile of books waiting to be perused and simply haven't had the time to get around to Dad's old books on top of those I am very interested in myself.

My mother died three years after my father and my sister followed her a few months later in 2007. She died from cancer that she had known about for some time but never informed me. Her only sibling, I was not told of her death until after her funeral. One of my cousins was charged with telling me. All in all a very cruel experience to overcome, particularly as there had been a total of four deaths of close family members in five months, and my husband was very ill and had left his job in India as a result of the illness.

Fast forward 17 years from my father's death. In December 2020 I had a dream in which my father had lawyers present at our old family home as he was making a new will. I asked if things were being shared equally with my sister as she was present in the dream too. I gathered she was getting her share in March 2021 but I would get mine a little later. Then Dad apologised to me for being rude and dismissive, he added that nobody deserved to be treated like that. Narcissists don't apologise and it was amazing to have a dream in which he did so even if it was 17 years down the track. Then he told me he was selling books to raise money. I stated that I hoped they weren't my books and he responded they were his.

After waking from this dream it occurred to me that I should have gone through Dad's books by now. I had been concerned about the money I was spending publishing my *Waking Wisdom* trilogy and wondered if Dad was trying to tell me something. Over the next month or so my intuition nagged at me about Dad's books and I felt I was being told to check them out. I hadn't thought that they were possibly valuable but the dream had made me aware that there might be a point to looking into that. My girls won't bother checking them when I die and they might miss one or two that will bring a bit of money in. Plus, I recalled that some sounded interesting. So, I began sorting through them. I found an online site that gives some idea of value. It has been a slow business as any avid reader understands when sorting books a great deal of time gets lost in actual reading. There are some amazing books I discovered, such as: *The Alchemists, Founders of Modern Chemistry, Oriental Magic, Myths of Mexico and Peru, A Search In Ancient Egypt* and *The Initiate in the Dark Cycle* just to name a few. None are worth a great deal though. Among the last few to come off my shelves was a slightly battered copy of *Swedenborg's Minor Works*.

When I opened this book there is a signature of Alfred Deakin dated 3rd of July, '77. I thought to myself that someone had bought it in a second-hand bookstore in 1977 and signed it. Then I turned to the next page where it had been signed again, this time more neatly, Alfred Deakin 3rd July, 1877. A shiver ran right through my body from head to toe. Alfred Deakin was the second prime minister of Australia and concerned with Federation. Immediately I started doing some online research of Alfred Deakin. He would have been nearly 21 years old when my book was signed. I found a great source that informed me of his early interest in spiritualism and in the mystics. The poet William Wordsworth and Swedish scientist, philosopher, theologian and mystic Emanuel Swedenborg had become a passion in his early years. The writer of a blog about him told me that 1877 was around the time Deakin became interested in Swedenborg and his intense interest lasted a few years into the 1880s.

Of course, this has only just happened as I am finishing off this book of mine and about to send it to be published. I am as yet unaware if the signature can be authenticated as Deakin's, and although he kept journals I don't know what is available from his earlier years for comparison. Deakin lived in Melbourne where my father haunted bookstores and second-hand auctions. What really makes me laugh though is the sense of humour that spirit has. My sister was to get her share of the new will in March 2021, the very time I discover the Swedenborg book. For me, rather less than spiritually it shames me to say, her share consists of, 'ha ha you missed one.' A little unfair perhaps as she has been very helpful to me on more than one occasion since she died. We get on much better now than when she was in mortal frame. Whether a book of financial value or not this little book is a gem. As a family heirloom it will be appreciated for the tale that comes with it which I hope Emanuel Swedenborg and Alfred Deakin also enjoy. Naturally, I must now read the book too. I wonder if it supports any of my understandings of wisdom, love and consciousness. Perhaps in *Waking Wisdom* book two I can inform as to the validity of the signature.

This is an appropriate place to end this book, at a point where it has been made apparent how powerful dreams can be. The altered brain-wave state of dreaming is a vast storehouse of information, love and guidance, and it is a spiritual tool that is universally available to all regardless of dogma, race or creed. Dreams of great clarity and lucidity are often the place of reunion with deceased loved ones. Dreams provide guidance, precautionary views or predictive views of the future. Dreams solve problems, gift inventions and even compose music and poetry. Give dreams a chance to perform their magic in your life.

* * *

Stop the Press: I showed the signatures to Alfred Deakin's biographer and she confirmed them to be genuine.

Kim Parker is a shamanic practitioner, author and dream worker. She channels mystical poetry and uplifting spiritual messages. She has had a lifetime of extraordinary experiences. She shares some transformational tales here to lovingly illustrate the rich and sacred wisdom to be harvested by investigating the strange and wonderful.

Kim is also the founder and facilitator of an online group called GOSH, an acronym for gatherings over strange happenings. This provides a safe space for people to discuss their experiences and interests in the realm of the paranormal.

Kim lives with her family and pets near Lake King in East Gippsland, Victoria, Australia. She enjoys walking and photography and bakes a mean cheese cake.

www.wakingwisdombooks.com

www.ingramcontent.com/pod-product-compliance
Lightning Source LLC
Chambersburg PA
CBHW072335300426
44109CB00042B/1627